ALSO BY SHANE MCCRAE

POETRY

Cain Named the Animal

Sometimes I Never Suffered

The Gilded Auction Block

In the Language of My Captor

The Animal Too Big to Kill

Forgiveness Forgiveness

Blood

Mule

PULLING
THE CHARIOT
OF THE SUN

A MEMOIR OF A KIDNAPPING

Shane McCrae

SCRIBNER

NEW YORK   LONDON   TORONTO   SYDNEY   NEW DELHI

SCRIBNER

An Imprint of Simon & Schuster, Inc.
1230 Avenue of the Americas
New York, NY 10020

First Scribner hardcover edition August 2023

SCRIBNER and design are registered trademarks of The Gale Group, Inc., used under
license by Simon & Schuster, Inc., the publisher of this work.

For information about special discounts for bulk purchases, please contact Simon &
Schuster Special Sales at 1-866-506-1949 or business@simonandschuster.com.

The Simon & Schuster Speakers Bureau can bring authors to your live event.
For more information or to book an event, contact the Simon & Schuster Speakers
Bureau at 1-866-248-3049 or visit our website at www.simonspeakers.com.

Manufactured in the United States of America

1 3 5 7 9 10 8 6 4 2

Library of Congress Cataloging-in-Publication Data is available.

ISBN 978-1-6680-2174-3
ISBN 978-1-6680-2176-7 (ebook)

For Melissa

Every story is by definition a resurrection story.

—CATHERINE PICKSTOCK

I could not run without having to run forever.

—SYLVIA PLATH

MY GRANDMOTHER

THE SIDEWAYS RAIN

B efore I saw it cascading across the fabric store parking lot, tumbling across the fabric store parking lot like a gif of two impossibly small gray birds fighting that has been copied and pasted a hundred thousand times, reeling through the air above the fabric store parking lot, the four hundred thousand wings overlapping, intertwining, each of the paired birds seeming to flap away from its opponent even as it attacks its opponent, I hadn't known rain could fall sideways. I was seven years old. Maybe I was nine years old—any age after my grandparents kidnapped me and took me to Texas. I was three when I was kidnapped, any age. The day must have been a Saturday or a Sunday because when my grandmother and I stepped from the fabric store we were shocked at how dark the day had become, so it must have been midday, me not in school. Unless it was a summer day. Usually whenever we shopped for fabric store things, whenever my grandmother shopped for fabric store things, we went to a Michaels in a strip mall down Highway 183 just far enough for the strip mall to seem alien, impossible to get home if I were ever left there, but on this day we had gone to a fabric store I had never seen before, its name a blank stucco edifice to me now. Am I misremembering it?

MY GRANDMOTHER—MY MOTHER'S mother—was white, like my grandfather and my mother; my father was black. When I was a child, whiteness and blackness weren't facts *about* me— whiteness was a wheat field I stood in; blackness was a pit somewhere in that field, hidden by the somehow taller stalks growing from it, taller insofar as they grew from the fathomless bottom of the pit to match the height of the other stalks in the field, those growing from the near and solid earth. My grandparents and I lived in a yellow brick house, its color and composition indicative of a whimsy be- longing to none of its inhabitants, though my grandfather repainted it occasionally, always yellow, and even if he hadn't known about the yellow brick road when we first arrived at the yellow brick house, his family had been poor when he was young—no movies, few books, if any books—eventually he must have repainted the bricks yellow with *The Wizard of Oz* in his head, a yellow brick house in Round Rock, a suburb of Austin. We lived in a house funnier than the per- son who made it funny was. Over the next few years, assuming I was seven the day I first saw rain fall sideways, over the next few years, our house was up for sale, and while our house wasn't selling, my grandmother would become an independent real estate agent and a real estate appraiser. At first she would work as a real estate agent for an agency with a brown and yellow corporate color scheme, then she would work for an agency with a red and white corporate color scheme, like the colors of the H-E-B grocery store sign, except the H-E-B sign was red with a ring of white between the red of the body of the sign and the sign's red border, but I imagined white at the edges of the sign, or deep inside the sign—I imagined white as the finishing touch to every colored thing. The first time she took me to the H-E-B, near enough to home that I could walk home if I were left there, but far enough away from home that I would give up on the way, after we had finished shopping, just after we had gotten into the Datsun, a 1981 desert-sand-colored Datsun 210 hatchback, to drive home, my grandmother told me H-E-B stood for Herbert E. Butts, and I thought that was hilarious, but the other day I read somewhere, or thought I read somewhere, that Herbert E. Butts did a significant amount of charitable work while he was alive. But was his name even Herbert E. Butts? Am I misremembering it?

The brown and yellow agency would become the red and white agency, and my grandmother would be swept up and carried by the change.

But she would never be rich, not on her own. But every once in a while she would try to get rich—like the time when, after we saw a story about the Cabbage Patch Kids craze on the news, I remember lingering shots of long, empty aisles where the dolls had been, me wondering whether the aisles were aisles in the local Toys "R" Us, she tracked down a lone Cabbage Patch Kid, a black boy doll named Fritz, then, using Fritz's tiny black body as a guide, she stitched her own dolls, white dolls, she called "Abbage Patch Kids," making copies of Fritz's birth certificate with the photocopier she had bought for her real estate business, but with both the *C* in "Cabbage" and the *X* in "Xavier," the name of the creator of Cabbage Patch Kids, whited out. She tried to sell the dolls at a garage sale we had a few weeks later, then again at a garage sale we had a few years later, then she gave up. Abbage Patch Kids by Avier.

I n our dining room, on the wall next to the passage to the laundry room, a portrait of my grandmother as a high school senior hung, opposite the kitchen. By the time the portrait was painted she had already been married and divorced. In the portrait, she looked like a young Elizabeth Taylor, not an eighteen-year-old Elizabeth Taylor, but an Elizabeth Taylor in her mid-twenties, though my grandmother's eyes weren't violet, but brown, and her hair was short and curly—an Elizabeth Taylor who stopped just short of being Elizabeth Taylor, in profile against a white, featureless background, gazing up at something slightly taller than her outside the frame. My grandfather was a painter, not professionally but as a hobby, but hadn't painted the portrait—he and my grandmother hadn't met when the portrait was painted. His specialty was realistic oil paintings of natural scenes. But on the wall perpendicular to the wall with the portrait, my grandfather's single experimental painting loomed, five feet tall and two feet across, a parody of a Jackson Pollock drip painting, its palette restricted to dark red and brown, and the paint piled thick, suffocating every inch of the canvas, both still and oozing down the canvas forever, but too slowly for its motion to be seen.

(Once, in the middle of the night, when I was about eight years old, I thought I saw the Devil in the laundry room just beyond where my grandmother's portrait hung. He had horns, a tail, and was holding a pitchfork, but his body was a void, outlined in crackling red and yellow static. I had snuck out of bed to get a glass of Kool-Aid, and when I turned into the living room, I saw the Devil emerge from the darkness at the back of the laundry room, maybe thirty feet away from me, on the other side of the living room, and as he slid forward he leaned first against the pistachio-green dryer, then against the pistachio-green washer next to it, then against the big wooden cabinet, big enough for me to hide in, next to the washer and dryer, and when he reached the doorframe he peered around it and into my eyes. I stepped back and blinked and he vanished.)

My grandmother's portrait hung perpendicular to my grandfather's parody. Between them stood our dining table, set always for six, though there were only three of us, but sometimes my mother, Denise—I called my grandparents "Mom" and "Dad," and my mother "Denise"—would visit from the other side of Austin, or from Dallas, or from San Antonio. The table had a chrome frame which held its glass dining surface in place, like a large windowpane, but all you could see through the glass was the giant chrome X made by the two tubes, each about the circumference of a dime, connecting and reinforcing the table's legs, and fixed a foot above the carpet, and beneath them the shallow butterscotch-candy-colored carpet. Nothing but the edges of the frame supported the glass itself; the table seemed as if it had been designed as a dare. We must have eaten at this table, but I don't recall us ever eating at this table, except I remember once I stood to go to my room, crying, the frame of the table cool against my belly through my thin T-shirt, my spaghetti with meat sauce only half-finished, I stood, but my grandfather must have shouted, "Sit down," because right away I sat down again, hard, and my grandmother, still chewing, said, "You're lucky. When Denise wouldn't eat her food I stabbed her hand with a fork."

MY GRANDPARENTS USED to tell me our house had been built on top of the largest network of caves in Texas, and the creaking I heard at night was the house slowly sinking into the caves, eventually, I thought, our house would fall into the caves and disappear. But don't worry, they would say—my grandmother would say—we'll be long gone before that happens. Don't worry, they would say—my grandmother would say—we won't live to see that happen.

The Unpopular Child

I went to Good Shepherd Lutheran School for kindergarten and then skipped first grade. Or, I went to Good Shepherd for first grade, after I skipped kindergarten. The latter story was the story I was told and I told others when I was a child, but I have at least one memory of kindergarten—in it, I'm building a fort out of large red cardboard blocks in a large room with five or six other children. But I also remember the first day of first grade. I remember sitting at a desk in a different, smaller room—but located, in my memory of it, immediately adjacent to the room in which I might have attended kindergarten for a day—humming a sound to myself I thought nobody else could hear, not a tune, but a single note, with my eyes closed, and I remember thinking, "This is great! I can make this sound and nobody can hear it! It's all mine," and I remember a teacher clearing her throat loudly and then telling me to stop humming. Either way, because I was considered to be developmentally ahead of other kindergartners or first graders—despite the humming, despite being a child who would do such a thing, or because I was a child who would do such a thing—I skipped a grade when I was five or six. (Can I know now whether I was gifted or just strange? Would a kidnapper be more likely to believe the child they have stolen is gifted? One would believe the child one has stolen, presumably at some personal risk, is valuable, right? But why do I suspect a kidnapper would be more likely to think the child they have kidnapped is just strange, and for that reason, in their estimation, less valuable than another child might be? They raised me, but I don't know what my kidnappers thought of me, except I know they disliked my blackness, and probably valued me less than they would have valued a white child. But they wouldn't have kidnapped me if I had been white—or, they might have, my grandmother might have, but for a different reason—because they kidnapped me to get me away from blackness, thereby making a place for blackness in their home.) I was switched from Good Shepherd—situated, as I remember it, a few miles from my house amidst trees at the edge of land that would eventually become a country-club-esque development called Lago Vista, in which for years my grandparents would unprofitably own a stubbly, dry acre—to a public school for second grade.

When I started second grade—at Forest North Elementary, which was across the street from my house, although by "across the street" I mean across the street *and* down a long driveway that was really a street in its own right, across the street and down a long driveway that crossed over a body of water that was a narrow creek where it disappeared under the driveway and was a large, wide pond where it reappeared—when I started second grade I was six, and thus younger than the other second graders. This might have been an accident owing to the nearness of my birthday to the beginning of the school year, or it might instead have been, as my grandparents claimed it was, the result of their decision to allow me to skip either kindergarten or first grade. Either way, when I started second grade I was both younger and taller than my peers. I was also unpopular—possibly the least popular child in the second grade. At the time, my unpopularity seemed unreasonable to me—after all, I looked like a young Michael Jackson, and Michael Jackson was popular—but now I understand my unpopularity was, from the beginning of my time at Forest North, inevitable. After all, I looked like a young Michael Jackson, and almost all the other kids looked like themselves, which is to say they were white.

One day, it was a library day, I think it was the first library day of the year, and so my first library day ever, since we hadn't had library days at Good Shepherd, I broke away from my class and found the books about World War II, and took a few of those books to a table in the center the room, the library was one big room, and there, after studying the Allied and Axis fighter planes, and after lamenting what seemed to me the general superiority of the P-51 Mustang over all German fighter planes, I took a black marker from my pencil bag and drew swastikas all over my white T-shirt. As I took the books back to the shelf, the teacher, whose name I've forgotten, noticed my shirt, and grabbed my sleeve, and asked me, "Why would you do this?" and ordered me to the principal's office, whose name I *do* remember, Mrs. Hood, and who at the time seemed like both a god and a statue to me, and whose hair was a tall cloud of golden steel, where the secretary told me to go home and change. So I walked home. After I explained to my grandmother why I had been sent home, she said—it was a contained exclamation—"That's ridiculous. They can't send you home for that." All around them, my grandparents saw things being done by people who, in their estimation, for moral reasons, or for reasons of biological inferiority, or both, shouldn't have been able to do them, and this made my grandparents, especially my grandfather, but my grandmother, too, both angry and sad—though their sadness usually looked like seething anger. My grandmother called the school and didn't send me back that day. At no point—neither at school nor at home—did anyone say a word to me about the Nazi genocides, or Nazism, even. After he got home from work, my grandfather beat me for ruining the shirt.

By the time she turned twenty-eight, my grandmother was six months into her fifth marriage. My grandfather was my grandmother's fifth husband. She had married her first husband when she was fifteen, in 1949 or 1950—I'm not sure how old he was, but probably fifteen or sixteen; they were in the same year at the same high school in Walla Walla, Washington. My grandmother always insisted she had been the most popular girl in her high school, and had married the most popular boy, the school's star athlete, captain of the football team, also the quarterback, captain of the basketball team, who later went on to become a professional football player and a millionaire. They were friends with everybody, even the one black student in their school, a boy their age. On weekends, they would drive him to the next town so he could date—there were no black girls in Walla Walla, and he couldn't date a white girl. According to my grandmother, not long after marrying, she and her first husband divorced at the insistence of her husband's coach—at the time, it was widely believed that sexual intercourse sapped an athlete's strength.

How could there have been no black girls in Walla Walla?

I've always thought of my grandmother's first husband, who

died in 2003, two years before my grandmother, as a shadow grandfather, though I never met him, never even spoke with him on the phone—even though if he and my grandmother had stayed married, my mother, who is the biological daughter of my grandmother's third husband, would never have been born. How else to name the relationship between us? My grandmother spoke of him so often—though she never said anything particular about him other than that he was popular, and a star athlete, and eventually became a millionaire; I don't know whether he was kind, or funny, or smart—she spoke of him so often, especially after she divorced the man I grew up calling my grandfather, that she established a relationship between us, even though she probably never mentioned me during the phone conversations they had in the last few years of his life. After fifty years, talking to each other again, my grandmother glowing like a girl again, she and my shadow grandfather, my first grandparents, as they had talked when they were young and together in the front seat of the sky-blue Ford convertible she always mentioned, though she never said who owned it, taking the first black boy my grandparents ever pitied to find love in the nearest place love was available, which wasn't where they lived.

I say my mother was the *biological* daughter of my grandmother's third husband because my grandmother always said he was my biological grandfather. When my mother was two years old, my grandmother took her from my biological grandfather, she took my mother away and didn't tell my biological grandfather where she was taking her, as my grandmother would later take me from my father, kidnap me, and my mother didn't find her biological

14

father until she was sixty. Years after my grandmother divorced my biological grandfather, eleven years after, by then the man I call my grandfather had been married to my grandmother and raising my mother for eight years, when she was thirteen my mother was adopted by my grandfather, the man I still call my grandfather even though when I think of him I think of him as disowned, that I've disowned him. But is it possible to disown up? Whenever I've heard the word used, I've heard it used in reference to older people disowning their younger would-be beneficiaries. If it's possible, I disown him, and if it isn't possible, I've said I disown him.

My grandfather and my grandmother married when my mother was five, at which time he told her he would adopt her when she turned thirteen if she was good. Then he beat her until she was good. Then he just beat her.

M ost of the time, while writing this memoir, I've relied on my memory. Most of the time, while writing this memoir, I've believed this memoir to be *about* my memory, in memory of my memory. Every so often, however, I've had to do research in order to ensure accuracy. Because I write in memory of my memory, I write knowing that some of what I write will be inaccurate—insofar as each person, each self, is constituted of accumulated memories, each person is constituted of both accuracies and inaccuracies. But I try to be as correct as I can be with regard to other people where it is possible for me to confirm information about other people. I've only recently—yesterday—discovered that the story my mother and I were told about her early childhood, that my grandmother divorced my mother's biological father when my mother was two, is untrue. Having seen the divorce decree—for the first time yesterday, but I have a copy of it, and just looked at it again, but I've also looked at it at least a dozen times between the first time I saw it and just now—I now know my mother was a week shy of ten months old when my grandmother divorced her father (just as my grandparents told me I was eighteen months old when my mother gave me to them and they took me to Texas, whereas the truth is I was three years old when they kidnapped me). But the decree also includes, typed into a blank corresponding to the phrase "Disposition, names and ages of children involved," the following: "Defendant granted custody of the One child, a girl, age about 1 year, born during this marriage but is an issue of a previous marriage." In 2017, my mother, who had never seen this decree and had never been given an accurate and complete description of its contents, after long research of her own, found the man who, according to my grandmother, was her biological father—the man my grandmother divorced with this decree. She was sixty. He was still alive, is, as far as I know, still alive. The man who, according to this decree, was actually her biological father died in 2005. But I can't discover anything more about him, my grandmother dead, who left behind no journals, no letters, only photographs of her last family, she, my grandfather, and I, and photographs of her parents when they were newlyweds, and photographs of her parents with her and her siblings when her parents were young and she and her siblings were children, as if she had never had another family between her first family and her last. Since I am, in part, the story I was told about my mother, the story she was told, I can't erase the story. But I am not the story I was told. The bubbling sensation as your genes change beneath your skin.

We had driven to the fabric store early in the afternoon on a cloudy, dry day, and we emerged from the store a few minutes later in the night, in a storm. My grandmother and I stood underneath the awning, in front of the automatic sliding doors, and she said, without turning to look at me, "Have you ever seen rain like that before?" Then she lifted her purse almost to her face and bent over it, digging for the folded plastic hair protector she always kept with her. A few minutes earlier, not long, maybe ten minutes, we had walked through the automatic sliding doors and straight down a wide aisle that divided one half of the store from the other. Every aisle except for the dividing aisle branched from the dividing aisle at a ninety-degree angle. My grandmother had walked straight down the dividing aisle to the second-to-last aisle on the left; I had followed just slightly behind her. As she scanned the shelves, I asked her if I could go look for toys, since I had never been to this particular fabric store before, and even though I knew there probably weren't any toys, I didn't know *for sure* there weren't any toys, and even though she said, "I only came here for one thing, and it looks like they don't have it," she let me go anyway, and I took off running back to the dividing aisle.

WHEN I WAS A KID, I loved just about any kind of store except for fabric stores and hardware stores, each of which existed at the edge of my ideas about femininity and masculinity. At the time, I wouldn't have thought to compare the boredom I felt in hardware stores to the boredom I felt in fabric stores, but now I understand I found the former considerably more boring than the latter, though I thought of myself as a manly boy. At least fabric stores were colorful. At the time, I wouldn't have said so, but as a child I thought of femininity as colorful, whereas I thought of masculinity as a grayish blur of violence.

I RAN DOWN the dividing aisle, pausing briefly every few strides to examine first the aisle to my left, then the aisle to my right for any signs of toys. Hardware stores never tricked me into thinking I had seen toys at the far, narrow edge of an aisle; fabric stores offered illusion after illusion—reds, and blues, and yellows, and greens all along every aisle, each new wall of many colors at first glance seeming to be a wall of toys. Illusion after illusion. I ran from illusion to illusion from the back of the store to the doors, and if the storm had already come I didn't see it through the glass of the wide, automatic doors, but I stopped just after the aisle nearest the doors, just after the last illusion, and turned, and ran back up the dividing aisle to my grandmother, rebuilding the illusions, though I knew they were illusions, seeing them again but as if I hadn't seen them before.

A kidnapping is a conversation between adults in the midst of which a child screams.

The child screams. The child kicks and cries. The adults who have taken the child can't hear what the adults from whom they have taken the child are shouting, so focused are they on the child's noises, the child's violence.

They must calm the child. If the child is young enough—a toddler, say—and the child knows and loves his kidnappers—if they're his grandparents, say—and his kidnappers have promised him better versions of the toys he was forced to leave behind, and they've promised him he'll see his father again soon, eventually he stops screaming, kicking, crying. If his grandparents quickly give him sweet things, like ice cream, and then slowly, not right away, but soon after they take him, over months, then years, suggest his father didn't want him, and his father's family was dangerous—if they tell him, say, that though he might not remember it, one of his father's relatives, an aunt, or a cousin, on drugs, an animal, had two Christmases ago broken into the apartment in which he lived with his mother, and stolen all his presents—eventually he hates his father and his father's family, eventually their faces, but not only their faces, but their voices, also, and their names, also, and their whole selves fade from his mind, and the kidnapped child doesn't know anymore how many people are in his father's family, but he knows a relative of his father stole his Christmas presents, and so he knows his father's family has at least two people in it, and one is a thief. But not only did his father not want him, not only did his aunt, or his cousin, steal from him, but also everyone who looks like his father, everyone with dark skin, and dark, curly hair, and dark eyes, everyone who looks like the kidnapped child, but darker, is just like his father and his aunt, or his cousin—they're all criminals, and none of them loves him. If he is told all these things, the kidnapped child will hate the people his kidnappers hate, but not the way they hate—their hatred is a still blue pond in which their faces are reflected; the kidnapped child's hatred will be an opaque, gray, swelling ocean upon which no image can rest. Their blue water is the white skin of water, across which runs the white path of the chariot of the sun; his gray water is black. He pulls the chariot of the sun across the sky above the water through clouds so thick and dark he can't see the chariot behind him, though its heat reaches through the clouds and scorches his back, though he thinks he is running from the thing he is pulling.

Past illusion after illusion, I ran up the central aisle of the fabric store, the dividing aisle, back to my grandmother. And when I complete the motion in my mind, at the end I run into her arms. She is wearing jeans and a white long-sleeve turtleneck and gold hoop earrings, and her arms are wide open and I almost leap into them. The open arms and the leap I remember from I don't know how many movies, the jeans I remember from my grandmother's life, though I'm not sure she ever wore jeans when I was a child, the turtleneck I remember maybe from a music video, but I can't remember which one, but I'm pretty sure whoever was wearing the turtleneck in the video was wearing it ironically, and the hoop earrings I remember from eventually—from years later, when my grandmother was dying.

But my grandmother and I weren't often physically affectionate. Over the years, we showed our affection by continuing to speak to each other. Most of our conversations after she and my grandfather divorced were about my grandfather, or my shadow grandfather, or how little money we had. Most of our conversations before she and my grandfather divorced were about her teenage years, or her Austrian ancestry, that she couldn't help siding with the Nazis, she was loyal.

"What does 'Achtung' mean?" (I had seen the word in a *Sgt. Rock* comic book.)

"It means 'attention!' And when a soldier saluted another soldier, he would raise his arm like this and say, 'Heil Hitler!'"

"Like this?"

"Just like that."

I RAN BACK to where my grandmother was—but not back to her, back to the aisle where she was, slowing to a jog as I approached the aisle. Slowing to a walk, I turned into the aisle where she was. I walked back to my grandmother. She hadn't left the aisle. She looked as if she were searching the shelves near the far end of the aisle, searching intently, or inspecting them, tilting her head back so she could aim her eyes downward and see the products right in front of her through the inset lenses of her bifocals. But almost as soon as I turned into the aisle, she asked, "Are you ready to go?"

Years later, when I'm a teenager and my face is covered at all times by acne, my grandmother will often stand right in front of me, just an inch or two away, tilting her head back and inspecting my face as she inspected those shelves, not seeing what she was looking for, a handsome boy she might have loved when she was a girl—in the years during which she inspects my face, my grandmother frequently tells me I have "a nice butt" in such a way that the sexual implications of the remark hover unsteadily between us; from the first time she makes it, she defends the remark by saying something like, or sometimes the exact phrase, "What? I can look"—but seeing, instead, my face, my seething pores, my black face.

When I'm three years old, my grandparents kidnap me. For most of my life, I've not known what to call what they did—growing up, I never thought to call it "kidnapping." And my mother, whenever she explained to me why I was living with my grandparents and not with her, which she did almost every time I saw her, explained with the gentlest words possible, but also quietly, her voice at the edge of a whisper, so that what they did seemed like a normal thing but also something I should never talk about to anybody. My grandfather had always wanted a son, and although he had physically abused my mother when she was a child, even though he was abusing her still, psychologically, when he told her he wanted to raise me, she believed that, because I was a boy, he would treat me differently. And so, when I'm three years old, my grandparents convince my mother that I would be better off living with them, and don't worry, she can visit me anytime she wants, and then my grandparents convince my father to let them take me with them on a weekend trip to a nearby lake, I think it was a nearby lake, wherever it was they said they were taking me couldn't have been far away, and the only trips I remember taking with my grandparents ended at lakes, or at least briefly featured lakes in the middle, after which my father intends to take me to Phoenix, Arizona, to spend a few days with relatives whose names I don't now know—why do I find the thought that I might have met them years later and not known they were the people I was supposed to have met when I was three, in the days that were instead the first days after I was kidnapped, unsettling? though my father might have mentioned them in the days before my grandparents kidnapped me, my family, though I might have said their names out loud.

Then my grandparents take me from Salem, Oregon, to Round Rock, Texas, without telling my father. He arrives at their house in Salem on Monday morning to discover the house has been stripped bare, even the curtains are gone. They tell my mother she will never see me again if she tells my father where I am—they will take me to Mexico and disappear forever. From the kidnapping on, nobody mentions my father to me except to tell me he didn't want me, but that's OK because he's black, and I shouldn't want him right back.

I grow up screaming I don't want him right back.

A SCREAM WILL TRAVEL as far as people choose to hear it, as far as people along the way it travels choose to hear it, sometimes across a country, sometimes not as far as the lips through which it passes—a scream can be its own ghost, unwilled. Decades after my grandparents kidnapped me, decades after I found him, my father told me the story of my kidnapping—not immediately, not the first time I saw him after finding him, not the next time I saw him after finding him, not while I lived with my grandmother still, then not while my grandmother was still alive, then not while I might be mourning her still—not the story of the kidnapping itself, a kidnapping can be a hole in the middle of the story of itself, so often is a hole, rather than strangers pulling up next to a child in a parking lot, the door of a van sliding open, not the story of the parts he didn't see, my grandmother dressing me for the trip, my grandmother holding my hand as she walked me from the front door to the car, not the drive to the airport, not the flight, the plane seeming to ascend too steeply, then slipping backward for a moment just after takeoff, my grandmother thinking she was going to die, me laughing, ecstatic, an event she talked about many times when I was a child without, of course not, once mentioning she was kidnapping me when it happened. My father told me the story of my kidnapping as he experienced it—rushing to my grandparents' house after he couldn't reach them on the phone the morning they were supposed to have brought me back to him, even from the street the house looked empty, he could see the house was empty through the windows from the street, still he crossed the front yard and pressed his forehead against a window and stared into the house, making a tunnel with his hands, one on either side of his face, so he could more clearly see the enormous nothingness pouring from the house. Decades later, in the midst of a stretch of months during which white Americans publicly acknowledged the mistreatment of black Americans by police, my father explained why he hadn't asked the police for help finding me, which was for the same reason he couldn't ask the police for help with anything else. A story will travel as far as people want to hear it.

The Wish

When I say it in my head, it sounds obvious, but, still, it strikes me as something I must write down: I don't remember when I started blocking painful memories, painful memories and memories of things I couldn't understand, painful memories, memories of things I couldn't understand, and memories of events, of people, I couldn't integrate into my idea of who I was—which idea, of course, I was both defacing and creating whenever I blocked memories. But I must have been young. For years, decades, I've assumed I must have started blocking memories when my grandfather started beating me, or maybe soon after—maybe with the third or fourth beating, or however many beatings it takes to convince a boy, a toddler or just after, that the only way for him to defend himself is to attack his own mind. *Just* now—as I was thinking about the events leading up to my kidnapping, the lies my grandmother, her alone, must have told my father, since my grandfather, who, when he discovered my mother was pregnant and discovered the father was black, grabbed a hunting rifle from the wall and had to be wrestled to the ground by his older brother, wouldn't have spoken to my father, since my grandfather was the sort of man who might kill a person to whom he nonetheless wouldn't speak—just now I realized I just as likely, maybe more likely, started blocking memories in the weeks following my kidnapping, and at least partly as a result of my kidnapping, and I want to say entirely as a result of my kidnapping, though I'm sure that isn't true. I want to say I started forgetting my life only because I had been taken away, physically removed, from my life. I want to say nobody could have hit me hard enough to make me forget my life with my father, though my grandfather started beating me in the weeks following my kidnapping, in the days following my kidnapping. But it would be just as true to say my grandfather couldn't hit me hard enough to stop me from eventually calling him "Dad."

A father is more a wish than a man.

The White Rocks:
The Body in the Dump

The neighborhood I lived in, when I lived in Round Rock, was large and unstable—most of the houses seemed old, although I think now they seemed old only in the way all structures, except for those they see rise before their eyes, seem old to small children, but every few years, and more likely it was every year, sporadically, construction would begin in a corner of the neighborhood I hadn't known existed, and sometimes I would come across empty fields that had been prepared for streets and houses, but the streets and houses hadn't been built. In one of these fields, which was otherwise scrub bushes and dirt, both brown, just a few yards past where the street ended and the field began, I discovered—I was about seven years old, maybe eight, and it was summer, and I had been biking aimlessly through the neighborhood, and had decided to turn down a street I hadn't explored before—a dump, I guess that's the word for it, and probably there *is* a word for it I don't know, and I would call it a quarry if it weren't so small compared to the other quarries I've seen. I discovered a dump full of mounds of small, just about the right size to throw at somebody, white rocks. Each mound was maybe three or four feet tall.

It seems unlikely that I actually did everything I remember doing on my first trip to the dump. But that phrasing is misleading—really I only did one thing, one strange thing, but the strange thing was strange enough that it would seem to have required some time away from the dump in order for me to work up the resolve to do it, as well as some time to plan it. Although what planning would it have required? And maybe it was exactly the kind of strange thing that can only happen spontaneously. One way or another, after having determined when I would be least likely to be seen or after having thought about nothing but the thing itself, the thing I had just resolved to do and knew I would in the next few moments do, I leaned my bike against a mound at the edge of the dump, I made my way to a mound in the middle of the dump, and I took off all my clothes. Then I climbed the mound and lay down.

Although I know I didn't put my shoes back on before I climbed the mound, in my memory I put my shoes back on before I climbed the mound. I think I'm inventing this, however, because when I try to picture the shoes, I see brown wingtip oxfords like my grandfather used to wear, I see myself naked wearing my grandfather's shoes, which are much too big for me, and my skin is almost as pale as the rocks. I'm not sure whether I was wearing shoes, or how pale my body was, whether I was almost the color of the rocks, whether a person would use the same word to describe the color of my skin and the color of the rocks, even though they would mean a different color, how could a person be as white as white rocks, the same

31

white, but I remember clearly the hot, sharp rocks I laid my body upon, and the biting ants that rose from beneath the rocks to cover my body, and I remember I leapt from the mound, panicked and suddenly ashamed, and danced to shake the ants off, and struck myself to knock the ants off.

The White Rocks: The Fish

The fish rotted on the white rocks in the morning sun.

I couldn't identify the fish. I knew the rocks: quartz. I loved rocks, and I had already started my collection. In a few months, I would find a small pile of sulfur in the shadow of a scrub bush, on a hill in a corner of the neighborhood that hadn't been developed yet, although excavators had started trenches.

The fish rotted on the quartz in the morning sun. A week or two ago, the neighbors—three houses to the left of my house, just around the corner—had landscaped a four-foot-by-six-foot rectangle of white quartz between the sidewalk and their lawn, and now dozens of silvery fish, each about eight inches long, glistened and bled on the rocks in the sun.

I didn't know where the fish had come from.

I can't say now where the sun rose in that neighborhood, my neighborhood in Round Rock, but about half a block south, I think, of the fish, a narrow creek divided the small block of familiar houses from the endless tangle of strange houses. Near the bridge, southwest of the fish, the creek shallowed and widened, and seemed mostly dead. But directly south of the fish, the waters were deep and occluded, and rough with catfish. And I imagined, staring at the fish, that they had slithered vengefully, or had been scooped up and carried vengefully, from that deep water to this newly domesticated rectangle of earth.

Later that summer, the creek flooded, and the septic tank in my backyard overflowed, and my backyard became a muddy field, except the mud was shit, and I played baseball in the shit with the children of family friends who lived in one of the strange houses up the hill on the other side of the creek. The kids joined me in the shit while their father helped my grandparents scoop shit from the house.

The quartz were so white they couldn't be dirtied by the bleeding fish. But the fish smelled like death. But I didn't know what death smelled like, that I was smelling death, in particular, and when the septic tank overflowed I thought of the fish, even though the smell wasn't the same—the shit smell from the overflowed septic tank was so strong I thought my shit had mingled with shit from all over the neighborhood, and this universal shit now rose through the dirt and blackened the lawn, and I played baseball in the universal shit, and thought of the silvery fish rotting in the sun on the white quartz.

I can't remember how the day of the flood ended, but I know I played for hours in the shit, baseball at first, but then just running in it to not stand still in it, to not begin to feel like I should wash it off—I knew if I stood still in it I would start to think about how filthy it was, how filthy I was. But I remember how the morning of the fish ended. I ran home to tell my grandparents, who wouldn't come with me to look at them, and when I returned to the fish—I ran back to them right after my grandparents told me they wouldn't come with me to look at them—the fish were gone.

Criminality

After breaking into my new friend's house—by now it was maybe five in the morning? and he had promised he and I, he was an older boy, but I can't remember his name or what he looked like, except the sandy blond bowl cut I picture at the top of every child's face I can't clearly remember from my childhood, the bangs almost touching the darker eyebrows, sits on his head, the bangs swishing in an indoor breeze, because I can only picture him, not him but his hair, not his hair but the hair of every child I knew when I was a child and now can't clearly remember, I can only picture him indoors, maybe his hair is swishing in a breeze from a fan, or maybe he's shaking his head no. He had promised he and I would go together to break into a different house, a house he knew was never locked, if I came to his house early in the morning, before his parents were awake, together we would break into a house, and I'm not sure what I had imagined we would do next, whether we had even discussed what we would do next, but I was six or seven or maybe even eight, though the fog through which the memory gropes and stumbles seems like the fog of a six-year-old's mind, a six-year-old's simultaneously certain and unclear sense of what right and wrong are. I was probably six and all I wanted was to be a criminal, to find my way back to my father through criminality, though I hated him then and didn't know I wanted to go back to him, to get away from my grandparents, whose own criminality seemed to make pathways for them, sometimes *through* me but never *for* me—after breaking into my new friend's house and finding him and everybody else in the house asleep, though my new friend had left a window unlocked, just like he had said he would, and now that I think about it maybe the unspoken part of the plan was that I would wake him up, but I couldn't. Seeing him asleep in his bunk bed, his brother asleep in the bunk below him, I had only met my new friend the day before, maybe in a hallway at school, or on the playground in front of the school, if he wasn't a student there, or in the forest, and I had been in his room the day before, and had seen the empty and unmade bunk bed then, and seeing him asleep in his bunk bed now, his brother asleep in the bunk below him, I saw I didn't belong in his house. Not just with my eyes, but my whole body saw it, a feeling like a shiver, like terror—even then I recognized it as a feeling of not belonging, of being trapped where I didn't belong, trapped in the quiet and sleep suffusing my new friend's house, and I turned and ran back to the window and climbed out. After breaking into my new friend's house I walked back home, where my grandparents were waiting for me, awake. The memory of the break-in seems absurd to me now. Did I really sneak out of my house at four-something in the morning, walk farther from my house than I was allowed at six years old to go? (I'm almost sure I was six; I remember being most afraid as I walked home that my grandparents would know I had gone farther than I was allowed to go) and break into the house of a boy I barely knew expecting he and I would then break into someone else's house and, yes, I think steal things, but what things I don't think even then I tried to imagine—the point was to break into a house and steal things from it, and if you don't steal things all you've done is break into a house, and that's almost not doing anything at all, you're a few feet from where you were before and on the other side of a wall, and what's that? Nothing. But it's one of my few childhood memories of which I've been conscious my whole life, one of my few childhood memories of which I *have* memories. When I got home, my grandparents were awake and waiting for me. But they hadn't called the police—one of them, almost certainly my grandmother, woke at four-something in the morning and discovered I wasn't in the house, but didn't call the police, but instead woke the other one, and they decided to wait. As I crept terrified back into the house—I had snuck out the window of the guest room, which was across the hall from my room, and now I climbed back into the house through the same window, but the lights were on and I knew my grandparents were awake—all I could think about was the trouble waiting for me. But when I return to the memory, mostly I think about how strange it was that my grandparents didn't call the police. But it wasn't strange at all. The child who had disappeared an hour before had disappeared years before. If my grandparents had called the police, the police might have found me.

A BLOCK FROM MY HOUSE, step out the front door and if you walk straight forward, down the two steps from the porch to the walk made of dusky golden to ruddy pebbles held together by something like honey-colored cement, a substance I haven't seen anywhere since my childhood, but the walk curves almost immediately to the left, but if you walk straight forward through the grass, be careful, you'll kick an anthill, the yard is full of them, and the ants, fire ants, but not always, and anyway every kind of ant in Round Rock bites, you'll send some of them flying in every direction, but some of them will cling to your kicking foot, and some of them will land in the grass ahead of you, and as you walk through the grass some of them will grab and cling to your feet, and if you walk straight forward through the grass, panic will catch you before you reach the street, Broadmeade Avenue, pain climbing from your shins just above your ankles to your calves, the ants know to climb, toward what? like they have a goal, like they're headed for your mouth, your eyes, you'll have to stop walking and then for a few moments hop in place as you slap and brush your legs, your hands moving faster than your mind can tell them to move. A moment ago you stopped but now you're running forward as you hop and slap yourself, you're in the gravel at the shoulder of Broadmeade, you almost throw yourself into traffic but the pain has stopped. You stop again, look down at your legs, you're wearing white shorts, your legs the color of the patches of dead lawn your grandfather can't get rid of, but darker, you've stopped, pink welts like miniature anthills where the ants bit you, you turn your head to the right as you look up again, you turn your body to the right, and if you walk straight forward along Broadmeade, cross Queensland Drive and after Queensland there's one house left in the neighborhood, on your right, at the corner of Queensland and Broadmeade, if you keep walking straight forward, past the house and its backyard, a block from my house, on the right you'll see the forest where I hunted, when I was a child, maybe nine, probably ten, for marijuana plants among the bushes and the wildflowers. I had no idea what marijuana looked like.

HALFWAY UP THE HILL between my house and the convenience store at the end of Broadmeade, half a block from the convenience store, I stepped off the shoulder of the road and clawed my way into the forest, pushing through a gauntlet of branches that seemed both endless and only a few feet long, some of the branches I pushed aside, after I passed them, striking my back as they wobbled into place—every time I stepped into the forest I felt as if I had to earn the right to be in the forest. Once in the forest, I crawled around tearing plants from the dirt and trying to light them with my grandfather's barbecue lighter. Most of the plants wouldn't light—most were too alive to burn—but I just figured the plants that wouldn't light weren't marijuana, and tossed them aside, and started crawling again. Every so often a dry brown stalk *would* light, and I would squat in the dirt smoking it for the few seconds it stayed lit, feeling nothing, hoping I wouldn't be seen, but hoping I would be caught. By the time I was maybe nine, probably ten, my grandparents had started talking openly about moving, though they must have been discussing it between themselves for years before, the house had been for sale for a year, maybe two, a sign indicating as much staked in the lawn, which both they and I pretended I never noticed. I wanted to be caught and banished from the community so I could move to a hovel just outside the community like a rueful outcast so I could stay near the community, I was nine, maybe ten, and thought in impossibilities. It had taken me so long, my whole life, to make the few friends I had, and I felt certain I wouldn't ever make any more. For most of my life I've thought that was why the move from Round Rock to Livermore was so hard on me. What being raised by one's kidnappers means is that after we moved from Round Rock to Livermore, when the reason I found moving emotionally difficult, worse than just emotionally difficult, an unhealable injury, was obvious— because I was taken from my father when I was three, moving away from the people I knew, my few friends, and the place I knew when I was eleven reopened a long-infected wound—it didn't even once occur to me that I might feel anguished about leaving my few friends for any reason other than the leaving itself, even though I knew children moved away from their friends all the time, and adjusted to their moves all the time. What being raised by one's kidnappers means is I crawled through the forest tearing plants from the dirt for hours not only hoping to forget my life, to be swept into oblivion by a plant I wouldn't have known if I had seen it, but hoping also I would be exiled from my home so I could stay close to my home—being raised by one's kidnappers means not knowing how to have a home except by not being a part of it.

I never saw my grandmother leave a store without buying something. Even if she had gone to the store looking for a particular thing and hadn't found it, still she would buy Dentyne or Tic Tacs on her way out. On our way out of the fabric store, she approached the cashier with no basket and nothing in her arms, and at the last moment, the moment before the cashier probably would have asked "Can I help you?" my grandmother grabbed a pack of Dentyne—only it wasn't Dentyne, but a brand I can't now remember, though I remember it was marketed as medicinal, but I can't remember its name, and eventually my grandmother did start chewing Dentyne, and in a more distant eventually, years later, my grandmother started chewing Trident, and in an even more distant eventually, some months or a year or years after she had started showing signs of Alzheimer's, though at the time I didn't know they were signs of Alzheimer's, but she was often angry and paranoid, and had begun hoarding, and eventually every buriable surface in her house was buried in garbage, but every so often I would find usable things, new things, products still in their packaging, a can of Campbell's Chunky Sirloin Burger soup, which had been my favorite soup when I was a child, but I didn't live with her anymore, a set of silver and gold glitter markers, two of each color, mixed in with the garbage, things that seemed to justify not throwing away or even moving the garbage, garbage about a foot deep on the floors, no path through it, so she slept on a couch in the living room, no path deeper into the house, but a path out through the back door, and next to the back door a bathroom, and the kitchen on the way, but even so the kitchen counters were buried three inches deep, eventually, after she had started showing signs of Alzheimer's, my grandmother switched from original Trident to watermelon Trident—my grandmother grabbed a pack of the pre-Dentyne, handed it to the cashier, paid for it, took it and her change from the cashier, then stuffed it and her change in her purse as we walked to the door.

The Mexican Child

PART I

I 've been Mexican everywhere I've lived.

Most recently, I was Mexican at the corner of Eighty-Sixth and Broadway. A man leaning against a handrail in front of a building on the corner asked me a question in Spanish as I passed close to him. I turned my head to look at him and said, "Sorry, I don't speak Spanish."

"You don't speak Spanish?" As he said this, I saw a tiny, disappointed horse trot across his eyes, shaking its head, pulling a shadow bigger than the man's body and my body combined.

"No."

He asked me what I took to be his original question again, but in English. He was asking for directions to a place I had never heard of, and I apologized for not knowing where the place was.

I was least often Mexican in Oberlin, Ohio, where I lived before moving to New York—I think I was Mexican only once there, in a Walmart parking lot just outside the city limits. Everyone in Oberlin calls it the Oberlin Walmart even though it isn't actually located in Oberlin, but instead about a mile south of town. Every time I've been Mexican, except for the first time, somebody was asking me for help—a man was asking me for help when I was Mexican in Oberlin, but unlike the man in New York, the man in Oberlin didn't speak English—so every time I've been Mexican, except for the first time, I've both regretted not being Mexican and wished I were more obviously black.

I was Mexican in Iowa City a few times.

I was often Mexican in Salem, Oregon. In my most vivid memory of being Mexican in Salem, I had gone to the sports bar across the street from my apartment for dinner, and in the middle of the meal I stepped over to the bar to ask the bartender for more Coke. The man seated at the bar next to where I stood turned to me smiling a friendly smile and offered to buy me a drink, "one Mexican to another." I told him I was sorry, but I wasn't Mexican. Laughing, he said, "You *are* Mexican. You just don't know it."

And it's true. I'm a black American—I might be Mexican and not know it.

Probably I was Mexican when I lived in California at least as often as I was Mexican in Oregon. But I was a child then, and men I didn't know didn't talk to me as often, so when I was Mexican I didn't know it.

The first time I was Mexican and didn't know it, my grandparents and I were returning to Texas from a brief visit to Mexico. My clearest memories of what happened at the border are memories of my grandmother telling me, repeatedly, the story of what happened at the border, usually while we were eating, and sometimes while she was laughing so hard she began to choke and cough. Apparently, government agents—of which government, I don't know—stopped my grandparents at the border, and accused them of attempting to kidnap me, to smuggle me, a Mexican child, into the United States. After a few tense minutes, during which my grandparents tried and failed to convince the agents I wasn't Mexican, I spoke, and although I didn't understand what was going on, whatever I said was so obviously American the agents instantly realized their mistake, and let us back across the border.

My grandmother never told this story while she and my grandfather were still living together. By the time she felt free to tell it, I had forgotten the whole thing.

I remember now, though, a small bowl of fruit in the border checkpoint in which the agents stood. "That orange is in a foreign language," I remember thinking.

The Mexican Child

PART II

My grandmother divorced my grandfather when I was fourteen. We were living in California, where I possibly was most often Mexican and didn't know it. They told me they were divorcing in a restaurant like an Applebee's, but without all the pieces of local color decorating the walls to emphasize its status as a neighborhood restaurant, in a shopping center in which, thirty or forty feet from the restaurant, was also a laundromat where, months before, I had discovered the arcade version of *Bionic Commando*, so different from the Nintendo Entertainment System version my grandmother would later buy for me on a road trip from California to Oregon, maybe to find a new house. The not-quite-Applebee's was dark, and we sat at a booth in an especially dark, empty corner—me on one side of the booth and my grandparents on the other. As soon as we sat down, my grandmother said, "Your grandfather and I are getting a divorce."

"Why?"

"Because I found out your grandfather had an affair. With a whore."

My grandfather mumbled a protest against my grandmother's use of a word he considered vulgar, to which she almost shouted, "Well, that's what she was!" And she glared at him, her eyes unrecognizable, like two hands slammed on a tabletop, her eyes red like two palms slammed on a tabletop.

One day, while I was at school, my grandmother had pulled the sheets off the bed she shared with my grandfather to wash them, and another woman's bra had fallen to the floor. "And I knew right away it wasn't mine," she said over chicken-fried steak as my grandfather used the bathroom in a brighter corner of the restaurant, far from us. When she told me why she was divorcing my grandfather, I was surprised—all my life, I had thought he could do anything he wanted. But after a few long moments of silence, I realized: he had only ever done anything he wanted to me.

At the time, I thought the force of the rain itself pushed the rain sideways across the parking lot—I thought sideways rain was the hardest rain. It didn't occur to me that the rain was driven by the wind, and I don't remember feeling the wind as my grandmother and I ran, embarrassed, or hunching as if embarrassed, squinting as if trying to determine whether an object on the horizon was a threat, hunching and squinting because of the rain, to the car, but only the rain itself stinging my face, my forearms, not the wind driving the rain, not the fist behind the punch, because I have to live with the fist forever, as far as I can see into the future, in which I hope to become a professional baseball player, though I can't picture myself in that future except I can picture myself standing at home plate, crouching a little, with a bat in my hands, but not any other image of my hoped-for future life, not my face in the mirror after I've been beaten, not a single bloody nose, though once I woke in the night in a pool of blood, in bed, but my face in a pool of blood, not a mark on my face in the mirror, but my freckles doubled, more than doubled, by the flecks of dried blood on my face, not my face, not the inescapable fist, I have to live with it, not the wind driving the stinging rain, I have to breathe it to live.

The single conversation I remember having as a child with another child about my father I don't remember—I don't remember how the part of the conversation about my father, itself only a few words, started, or what was said after it ended, and so I don't remember the conversation, only a few words about my father surfacing, surely not from silence, and almost immediately disappearing again, possibly into silence. The conversation I don't remember happened on a patch of grass near the bridge over the creek in which I was forbidden to play, above the bridge which marked the boundary between my corner of the neighborhood, which was situated at an edge of the neighborhood, either the beginning or the end of the neighborhood, an entrance and an exit either way, and the enormous rest of the neighborhood, I was walking from the enormous rest to my corner, I felt harried at the time. A boy—I can't recall his name or his face, but he might have had sandy blond hair, and he might have been my age, six, maybe, seven, maybe five, and in my memory he looks small even though I also recall he was about my height, and I was at an age when older children looked huge in a way adults did not (I still remember how my first day at Forest North began. I was told to sit at what seemed one edge of the cafeteria in a line with other children in the second grade, and at the far edge of the room the fifth graders sat in their own line, a few students who had just arrived striding in slow motion toward the end of the line like giants patrolling a misty, distant border, beyond which mountains no taller than the giants hardened sometimes into definite, craggy shapes, and softened sometimes into clouds, as fog drifted imperceptibly across them. I thought I had never seen people so big before)—a boy asked me who my father was, and I told him I didn't have a father. The grass beneath my feet was some of it stiff and the color of white skin, the tan color of white skin, and some of it stiff but green still, but a dusty, faded green. If I was five, I hadn't seen my father for two years, and I couldn't picture him anymore, not even the shade of his skin, and I didn't remember what his voice sounded like, not even the sound of my name as he spoke it, and I didn't know his name. "Everyone has a father," the boy said. Some of the grass was the color of the boy's skin.

MY GRANDFATHER

THE COLD AIR

Before I saw it drift from my mouth, like my soul gone out of me, then pause midair before disintegrating, like my white soul gone out of me to die outside my black body, I had never seen my own breath. I was in our Datsun in my great-aunt's driveway in Shawnee, Oklahoma, twenty miles from Meeker, on the second day of my family's first Thanksgiving at her house. My great-aunt had wiry copper hair she wore in whorls high on her head, almost like a helmet in a highly stylized, low-budget science fiction movie, and though she wore glasses like my grandmother wore, and like my grandfather wore when he read the newspaper, she didn't resemble either of them. Two years in a row in the middle of my childhood—two years in a row, maybe I was nine the first year, maybe I was ten the second year, and the year after that I was gone, or about to be gone, we had moved to California, or we were about to move—my grandparents and I visited her for Thanksgiving. Like everybody I knew in the South, she had a large, mostly empty backyard, but unlike anybody else I knew, in her backyard was a big wooden spool. I spent my first Thanksgiving visit learning how to stand on the spool and roll it around the backyard as if I were rolling a log on a river.

The following Thanksgiving, as soon as we got to my great-aunt's house, I ran to her backyard to roll the spool. I climbed on top of it—with difficulty, though the spool seemed smaller than it had the year before—stood up, slid my right foot forward, so as to make the spool roll forward, and fell to the ground. Surprised and confused, I climbed the spool again, stood up again, slid my right foot forward again, managed to actually roll the spool—about six inches, maybe eight—and fell to the ground. I got up, tried to brush the cold mud from my jeans, but only smeared it, and inspected the spool—though I could see right away that nothing about it had changed, except that it seemed smaller—and as I inspected it, I thought back to the previous year, as I had done for most of the long car ride from Round Rock to Shawnee, but now I didn't recognize myself in my memories. The boy who had rolled the spool around the yard, whoever he was, had understood his body in a way I didn't understand mine, and now he was a year ahead of me—a distant speck on an enormous lawn, dying in patches, green in patches, happily rolling a gigantic spool—and I couldn't catch up to him.

EARLY IN THE MORNING on the second day of my first Thanksgiving at my great-aunt's house, my grandmother or my great-aunt, or my grandmother and my great-aunt together, had given my grandfather a grocery list and told us to go to the Piggly Wiggly, the only Piggly Wiggly I've ever seen in real life. I had stood in my great-aunt's driveway beside the Datsun while my grandfather warmed it up. My grandfather had told me to wait outside the car while he warmed it up and so I had waited, anticipating the warmth, until he motioned me in. But the air in the car was colder than the air outside the car—I realized then that whatever he meant by "warm up the car," the warmth was for the machine and not us—and when I exhaled I saw my breath. Before, I had only seen cold manifest in this way in movies, and as I watched the tiny cloud disintegrate, I felt I had entered into an unreal space, a space made glamorous by the visible decaying of my breath, in our Datsun in my great-aunt's driveway, twenty miles from the town my grandfather had grown up in and seemed ashamed to show me, sitting next to my grandfather who seemed to feel compelled to show me the town he had grown up in, his shame.

We sat in the car together, waiting for it to warm up.

D oes knowing another person mean knowing what they know? Not knowing the *things* they know, but having knowledge of particular instances of their knowledge? Not necessarily knowing everything they know, but some of it? If so, how much? My grandfather worked for IBM when I was a child—he was in his forties then, like I am now, but he was in better shape than I'm in now, an inch shorter than I am now, mustachioed, I never once saw his naked lip, and muscular, he had begun working out not long after my grandparents kidnapped me, and he had also purchased and begun restoring a late-'60s Triumph Spitfire, an open-top convertible, the outside of which he eventually made beautiful, the inside of which he never worked on, except to put a thin piece of particleboard over a hole in the floor on the driver's side—and my grandmother used to tell me he had helped with the development of the PC. But I can't imagine him ever having known anything about computers. But if he did know things about computers, and if knowing things about computers was a significant part of his life, did I know him? When I was a child, I didn't know where he had been a child. Even when he took me to see the house in Meeker, Oklahoma, where he had lived as a child, seemingly on an unhappy whim, I didn't know where he had been a child. I couldn't believe he had ever been a child at all, anywhere, and when one is a child isn't knowing more belief than knowing? Is that more true for kidnapped children? We didn't stop at the house, but drove past it, and as we drove past it I tried to imagine him in the house, him in his grayscale childhood, him as a toddler, him too small to hurt me. But I couldn't—I couldn't integrate the mythical time of his physical smallness with the real, crumbling house we passed. But I knew him well enough to know he wasn't happy to see the house again, though it had been his idea to visit it—I knew by the look on his face. I knew what the looks on his face meant as well as I knew anything.

My grandparents told me my great-aunt was my aunt, and that's how I know she was my great-aunt—I have to add a generation to what they told me when I was a child to understand what they told me. But I don't know whose sister she was—nobody ever told me that. But I think she was my grandfather's sister. And, early in the morning on the second day of my first Thanksgiving visit to her house, she and my grandmother sent my grandfather and me to the local Piggly Wiggly, the only Piggly Wiggly I've ever seen in real life. But just now I tried to confirm via Google that there is, or at least used to be, a Piggly Wiggly in Shawnee, and could find no trace of one. Does the self end where misremembering the self begins? Does it make any difference, if I forgot things in my childhood to protect myself from them, that I had meant to forget only the suffering self, not the whole self? But even if I had known I was destroying myself by forcing myself to forget things, I don't think I would have tried to stop forgetting. Did I kill myself to save myself? But I've been to a Piggly Wiggly once in my life, somewhere far away from my life, at least once, my life at least.

Anywhere we drove alone together, my grandfather and I drove in silence. But my grandfather and I almost never drove anywhere alone together, and maybe it would make more sense to say that whenever we drove anywhere alone together, we brought along the enormous, everyday silence that had grown between us or had always separated us, I would say *always*, I wouldn't say *had grown*, but always, it seems to me, began when my grandparents kidnapped me, when I was a toddler, and what do toddlers know about silences between people, though I've never felt the presence of an adult's silence as uneasily as I've felt the presence of a toddler's silence, the potential length and solidity of it, unending, unyielding, that a whole person might grow on top of it, and anyway I don't remember a single word my grandfather ever said to me except the last words he said to me, the last words so far, thirty years ago, and a few words he said to me at the end of an afternoon when I was small, lying on a couch in the living room alone, after, but probably not long after, maybe a few months, after my grandfather had cleared his pornographic magazines from the living room, after my grandmother had told him I was "starting to notice," I couldn't have been older than four or five, maybe not even four, after he had moved his magazines to I never figured out where, at the end of an afternoon, but the sun was still out, I was lying on a couch in the living room, alone, my pants down, under an afghan my great-grandmother had knitted, and my grandfather stepped from his bedroom into the living room, and he saw my pants were down— my great-grandmother's afghan was mostly holes, and I didn't understand how it kept me warm, but it did—I was small, and he walked to the couch, and looked out the big sliding glass window to see if my grandmother was in the backyard, but he didn't see her, I know, because she wasn't there, and she wasn't in the house, and he bent over me, and said the only words I remember him saying to me that weren't *goodbye*, a way of saying goodbye.

The Dogs

I wanted to let the dogs go, I'm sure I did. I'm sure I had wanted to let the dogs go, the neighbors' two black Labs, even as I led them from the neighbors' backyard through my backyard and into my garage; I'm sure I had wanted to let the dogs go even as I pulled the big door down—I probably had to jump to grab the rope to pull the big door down—and trapped them in the garage with me. I can't remember what any surface in the house in Round Rock, the first house I remember most of, felt like, not the carpet, not the walls, not the countertops, except I remember what the glass surface of the dining room table felt like, that it felt perfectly smooth, and so my hand stuck whenever I tried to slide my hand across it, that it felt like a trap, and I remember what the fraying, dirty rope my grandparents used to pull the garage door down felt like—it felt like rough, dry hay, but more solid than hay. I jumped to grab the rope, and pulled the door down. Could I have been four?

The dogs were as big as I was. They belonged to the family that lived in the house behind mine, whose yard was the only yard of the three yards bordering mine that wasn't sealed off by a six-foot-tall wooden fence. Instead, their yard and my yard were separated by a three-foot-tall chain-link fence with an unlocked gate. I had opened the gate and called the dogs to me; I had turned and walked away, and the dogs had followed me.

The dogs had followed me into the garage, and I had jumped to pull the big door down. The dogs were as big as I was, bigger, and shiny black—the dogs reflected the white light from the big fluorescent fixture back at the ceiling, increasing the whiteness that hung above me, but also becoming white where the white light both rested upon and bounced off their backs. I was four—I must have been four. I hadn't seen my father for a year. His particular shade of blackness had disappeared from my mind along with his face, and his voice, and his hands, but my grandparents had already taught me that blackness—not just my father's particular blackness, but blackness itself, all blacknesses combined in my own blackness—was the worst thing about me, though also incidental. I wasn't black the way my father was black—I just tanned deeply, easily in the Texas sun. When I was four, and five, and six, and however old I was before I stopped asking, my grandparents told me I didn't look like them because I tanned deeply, easily. Were they to return me to darker, cooler Oregon, to my father, maybe my blackness, their idea of blackness, would disappear from my skin just like his blackness had disappeared from my mind. I was four. The dogs had followed me. I grabbed an aerosol can from my grandfather's workbench and spray-painted the dogs green, just their backs, where the whiteness shining from above me met their blackness, one or two strokes each, crying. The dogs squirmed and barked, and my grandmother rushed into the garage from the house.

Later that day, my grandfather beat me.

Then he built a new fence.

The Popular Child

Soon after I started second grade, I discovered I was unpopular. This was a shocking discovery—like rounding a corner to find your favorite restaurant had not only closed forever the previous week, but had also been demolished—and I would spend the rest of my elementary school years searching for the life I lost when I lost my sense of myself as loved by everyone. Throughout my childhood, I was aware that at home I played the role of the child in a three-person family headed by two adults who themselves played the roles of parents. Never once did I feel unselfconsciously like the child of my grandparents, though I think they wanted me to feel that way, or would have said they wanted me to feel that way—after all, they encouraged me to call my grandmother "Mom" and my grandfather "Dad." Racism is impersonal, though it is wielded against individual persons. Whenever I overheard my grandfather commenting on what he perceived to be the inarticulateness of a black student-athlete being interviewed on the local news, whenever my grandmother whispered to me as she leaned over the cash box at one of our biennial garage sales, "Watch out for the Mexicans. They steal," I was reminded that I could not be their child, that my skin would not permit it. Such comments were almost always directed outward, at people they didn't know, but I was the target.

All of which is to say that though I understood the child in a three-person family headed by two adults would in most cases be the object of parental love, I never felt so certain of being loved as to be unmindful of whether I was actually loved. So I looked for love outside of my home, most often at school. And in fact, for the second half of my first day at Forest North, I *was* popular, or at least I thought I was—when you're a child, you know your social status immediately, and a day of popularity is deeply felt even in its midst—and so I felt loved. During my first recess, most of the other children in my class had arranged a soccer game; because nobody knew me, I was picked last for a team. But because nobody knew me, nobody knew I was strong. Late in the game—my team was losing, and would lose—when, as the result of an error either by someone on my team or someone on the opposing team, I found myself in front of the ball, immediately in front of my own team's goal, I kicked the ball as hard as I could toward the goal on the other side of the field. As the ball flew through the air, all the other children seemed to stop moving; no one on the opposing team dared to defend against the shot. A long second after the ball rolled into the goal, everyone on my team roared, and if they could have hoisted me onto their tiny shoulders, they surely would have. Then the game was over, and the two most popular boys in the second grade put their arms around my shoulders, and escorted me back to class, celebrating my might all the way.

But the next day, nobody knew me.

From the beginning of my second day at Forest North, after I had dutifully purchased two NFL-themed pencils for twenty-five cents from the vending machines near the front doors, sauntered to class, sat at my desk, and tried, in a jocular way, to get the attention of the boy sitting in the desk next to mine, only to be shunned in such a way that I could feel myself being expelled from jocularity forever, from the bewildering first moments of my second day, I was aware I was no longer popular, and probably never really had been. None of the other second graders responded positively to my attempts to get their attention, not even to my desperate efforts to remind them of my soccer field heroics. Instead, those who did acknowledge me admonished me to pay attention to the teacher, demonstrating a commitment to education apparent in them under no other circumstances. Their racism made them better students.

And it *was* racism—even then, I knew it was racism that had shoved me from the happy eminence I thought I had kicked my way up to. I hadn't noticed, during my first day at Forest North, that I was the only black child in my classes. Though I was, with regard to my grandparents, at every moment aware of my blackness—or, both more and less specifically, my non-whiteness—because I was being raised by white racists, I was always on the lookout for otherness in other people, not in myself. I was not yet fully aware I harbored both otherer and othered; I did not yet know I was hunting myself. Yet I right away was certain the sudden coldness I felt from my classmates had been engendered by racism—nobody told me so, but I didn't need to be told. Later, during recess, we all played a new game. One by one, the boys in my class—most vigorously, the boys who yesterday had put their arms around me—rushed into me as I stood in the center of a circle they had made and tried not to fall. From outside the circle, it must have looked like a strange but harmless modification of Red Rover, and with regard to my blackness, my non-whiteness, I was simultaneously too proud and too ashamed to cry for help to the teachers sitting on benches no more than thirty feet away. But inside the circle I felt as if I were facing down threats to my survival as a student at Forest North, and as a human being. Whoever knocked me down won—I could not win. The game was called Whites vs. Blacks, though I was the only blacks.

But I was sure, as one after another of my classmates rammed into me, even as one and then another of my classmates rammed into me and knocked me down, I was sure that if they gave me a chance to kick a soccer ball again, if they watched me closely and saw how far I could kick it, if they realized I could kick it farther than any of them, I would be popular again, I would be loved. All I had to do was wait for that chance. And so I had volunteered for Whites vs. Blacks. Here began my years-long celebration of my body. It was a revolt against my body.

My grandfather almost never drove me anywhere by himself—my grandmother drove me everywhere, almost everywhere. Most of the time, she was a quiet driver. Once, for reasons I don't remember anymore, our next-door neighbor, I don't remember her name, but she lived with her husband in a house made of white stones to the right of our house and had raised two sons who had moved out when I was four or five, and so I must have been six or seven when this happened, once, our next-door neighbor, as a favor to my grandmother, had driven me to tae kwon do class, and all the way to the not-yet-run-down dojo in the middle of the run-down strip mall, too far from home for me to walk home if I were left there, she had sworn and shouted at other drivers—I had never heard my grandparents utter such words!—and I was shocked and terrified, though not by the anger or the shouting, but by the words themselves. Most of the time, my grandmother was a timid driver. Only after an accident in which a dump truck slammed into our Datsun on the passenger side, where I was sitting, did my grand-mother decide to become a more aggressive driver—I might have been ten. She started flipping off other drivers, and she would do so by raising her hand as if she were about to ask a question, but with the back of her hand to the other driver, and shouting, "Read between the lines!" My grandfather drove as silently as that upraised hand.

MY GRANDFATHER AND I backed out of my great-aunt's driveway. My grandfather backed out of my great-aunt's driveway and I sat next to him, gasping in reverse, gasping outward, trying to make my breath reappear, but the car had already gotten too warm, we backed out, curving to the left as we did so, and then drove forward. On our right stood my great-aunt's house—yellow in my memory, but the house I lived in at the time was yellow, too, and how many houses are yellow?—and the houses of her neighbors, on our left a pale yellow field seemed to spread from the edge of the street to the horizon, but at the end of the street on our left, on the corner, a shadowy brown apartment building rose from the field, as if it were a bridge between the field and the intersection. In my memory, even the glass in the windows was brown. A few days later, my grandmother would tell me that my great-aunt owned that building, that she was a landlord, and its shadows would deepen—I assumed all landlords were rich, but how could my great-aunt be rich? Wouldn't I have known already if my great-aunt were rich? Wouldn't some telltale effervescence have spread from her life over ours if she were rich? If my great-aunt were rich, wouldn't I be able to distinguish my life from the life I was living? Wouldn't I be able to tell myself apart from me?

But wouldn't a person *have* to be rich to own a building in which other people lived? The house immediately to the left of our house in Round Rock was the only rental in the neighborhood. Unlike every other house in the neighborhood, it featured brief, curving stone walls that sloped from the roof at each corner and looked like wings if you imagine the wings of a bird on a government seal, but instead of being raised over the bird's head, they're pointing down, they curve outward as if the bird were shrugging to indicate it didn't have any pocket change, and they stop at the bird's feet. Families seemed to manifest whole in that house; I don't remember any families moving in or out. A few times, there were children my age, or nearly, but they were always markedly different from the other children I knew—a girl my age with a voice raspier than any boy's, an older boy with a collection of Japanese swords. I had a crush on the girl and felt ashamed, knowing her family was poor; I felt jealous of the boy, but my grandparents let me keep the short bokken he gave me just before he and his family vanished from the house. I thought everybody who lived in that house was owned by somebody else. I thought I was the only other owned person in the neighborhood.

If my great-aunt were rich, wouldn't I be able to tell myself apart from me?

The Game in Shit

Not long after my grandmother died—she died at the beginning of November 2005—my mother told me the mother of the children who lived in one of the strange houses up the hill on the other side of the creek had died, too, years before my grandmother. She had been killed by the cancer she was suffering from even as her three sons played in shit with me in my flooded backyard. I don't know whether my grandparents knew she was sick, but I didn't know she was sick. As her sons played in shit, her husband was in my house, running from room to room, helping my grandparents save what they could from the flood, then helping them clean. I don't know whether her sons knew she was sick, but her husband must have known. Their sons and I played baseball in the roiling shit in my backyard—we had a bat, I remember the bat, but I don't remember a ball. Instead, I remember each of us took a turn standing at an imaginary home plate a few feet from the fence at the southern limit of my yard while another of us pitched an imaginary ball toward the batter, and according to the timing of the batter's swing, those of us waiting to bat determined whether the batter had struck or missed the imaginary ball, and if the batter had struck it, how far it had flown. And so, again and again there was a long moment between the batter's swing and his dash for first base, which was also imaginary. During that moment, the two boys waiting to bat would determine how much running the batter would do. Was it a base hit? Was it a pop out? Again and again we had to think for a moment before we sent our friends running through shit, but again and again we sent them running.

Every so often, glancing down at the watery shit as I ran to first base, or from first to second, or from any base to any base, or to home, I thought of the fish bleeding on the white rocks in the bright, early summer sun. I thought of the fish, and as I thought of the fish I imagined I saw them, once or twice, floating up to the surface of the watery shit—they looked like the blades of butcher knives wobbling in the ripples. About ten years later, when I'm seventeen, my grandmother, already swimming in Alzheimer's, though she won't know for another ten years, will be told by a psychologist treating me to hide all our knives—I had developed the habit of tapping the tips of knives against my chest while swimming in my own confused thoughts. But when a fish popped up as I ran to first base, or from first to second, or from any base to any base, or to home, as soon as I saw it I blinked it away. Weeks before, I had realized, facing the impossibly clean, impossibly dry bed of quartz where only minutes before dozens of silvery fish had lain bleeding, that I had misplaced a slice of reality, or a slice of time, or both—the slice of reality, or time, or both in which the fish were removed from the rocks. Most of the beatings I suffered as a child

74

I don't remember. Some of them I know about now only because my grandmother told me about them a few years after she left my grandfather, and I was then able to fit them into a few of the holes in my memory; some of them I know about now only because I know the nimbuses of fear that obscure them in my memory. When I recall the fish now, eventually I also recall the blood on the white quartz, and the blades of butcher knives floating in the dark brown shit; eventually, the images blend together, and the blood on the rocks is not blood from dead fish, but blood from the knives themselves; eventually, I have to put some effort into returning the fish to the rocks. But what is remembering if not giving each bloody knife a body?

The brown apartment building my great-aunt owned squatted on the corner at the intersection at the end of her street. The building sat in its own shadow like an eye in the shadow of the bill of a baseball cap—the building's shadow seemed to cover the building, as if the sun in Oklahoma shone also from the earth beneath one's feet. My grandfather and I stopped at the intersection. My grandfather stopped at the intersection, checked, he must have checked, for approaching traffic, though as I write this I realize I can't remember him ever turning his head, which I know sounds ridiculous—parts of him I remember in motion, parts of him I remember from photographs, but the photographs occupy scenes in my memories as if they were living parts of the living scenes, but because the photographs are still the scenes are still. I don't know whether the scenes in which parts of him are still, in which parts of him are photographs—a head can be a photograph, a hand, a foot— are scenes in which he hit me, and I have pasted stillness over the violence, or scenes in which he didn't hit me, and I have stilled him to make them last. At the intersection, my grandfather turned his head to the left and then to the right to check for approaching traf- fic. At the intersection, my grandfather's head was still.

The street perpendicular to my great-aunt's street was empty, I could tell it was empty from fifty feet away, but my grandfather stopped at the intersection anyway because even if nobody was watching us the apartment building was watching us and it was owned by family, or he stopped because everybody stops at stop signs. My grandfather looked like the sort of man who wasn't afraid of anybody, he wore a fearless, expectant expression on his face, an angry expression, an expression that might have been a thoughtful expression on another person's face, not a daydreaming expression, serious, just over the boundary into worried, but the worry was worry he might appear thoughtful—being thoughtful being next to being sensitive, being sensitive being feminine—and so at every moment his expression retreated from itself, it couldn't be caught, pinned down, accused. We drove through the intersection. Behind us, my great-aunt's apartment building seemed to sink into the landscape like a head nodding deeply *Yes* into a chest, becoming the same thing it was before in the same place it was before, but seen differently, *Yes, go ahead*.

Past the intersection, what had been an empty field on our left filled with houses, not gradually but all at once, and I turned my attention to the houses on our right, where there had always been houses. Short, bare trees stood between some of the houses; between the other houses, nothing. After a few minutes we stopped at another stop sign at another intersection, and at the next intersection—an intersection with a stoplight—we turned left, and then immediately right, and pulled into the Piggly Wiggly parking lot. The store had the kind of automatic doors that swung away from the person attempting to pass through them, rather than the kind that slid apart, and the "In" sticker on the in door was chipped and peeling. I remember asking my grandfather, after we stepped into the store, whether I could look at the magazines on the rack about ten feet from the door, and then standing before the rack, thumbing through a *Family Circus* book, but I don't remember what happened in the space between the asking and the standing, but my grandfather probably just said yes—nothing horrible, nothing cruel. How narrow the spaces into which I've disappeared, how shallow the spaces into which a person can disappear, how dark the spaces.

The *Family Circus* book, as I remember it, was about the size and shape of an *Archie's Double Digest*, but I wouldn't be surprised to discover no such collection of *Family Circus* comics was ever published—for a few years, whenever my grandparents and I would go on road trips, I would read issues of *Archie's Double Digest* in the car. As I thumbed through the *Family Circus* book, I saw for the first time the comic in which the many meandering steps a child takes to reach a nearby person or thing are traced. The child—let's say the child is a boy—wants to hug his mother, who is in the next room, or he wants a glass of orange juice, which is in the kitchen, and so walks from his bedroom or the living room through the front door or the back door, wanders through his yard and the next-door neighbor's yard, plays with somebody's dog, hops in a puddle, etc., then returns to his house, and finally hugs his mother or drinks the juice. I don't remember the boy's goal precisely, and I don't remember all the details of his course clearly, but I remember the joke: A boy can become unimaginably lost. Even if he comes back home, he has been unimaginably lost.

I had asked my grandfather whether I could look at the magazines on the magazine rack not because I wanted a magazine, or even an *Archie's Double Digest*, but because we had no shopping protocol. Whenever my grandmother and I would go to the H-E-B together, we would split up, and she would shop for groceries while I gazed at toys, and eventually I would find something I wanted or I would get bored, and would run the length of the store perpendicular to the aisles, glancing down each aisle as I passed it, searching for her. I hadn't thought it would be safe to ask my grandfather for a toy, and I hadn't thought I could trust him to wait for me if I went to the toy aisle just to look, we didn't have a protocol, and so I had asked if I could stand by the door like a child selling cookies or asking for donations, like somebody else's child.

WE LEFT THE PIGGLY WIGGLY carrying something red. My grandfather left the Piggly Wiggly carrying something red. Or the packaging was mostly another color, but the product inside the packaging was red, and was represented by an attractively staged photograph, mostly red. My grandfather left the Piggly Wiggly carrying something red, but I can't picture him with a bag in his arms, guiding a Piggly Wiggly employee to our car, popping the hatchback, or instructing the employee to load the bag with the red thing into the trunk. And maybe there were other bags, maybe we bought other things, though since this was a trip to buy something, or a few things, my grandmother or my great-aunt had forgotten— though since we were having dinner at my great-aunt's house, surely she would have been the person who had forgotten whatever it was we had just bought—surely, since this was a trip to buy a forgotten thing or a few forgotten things, there wouldn't have been many other bags. Maybe the red thing was a can of cranberry sauce, I can picture my grandfather with a can in his hand, anything metal. What if my grandmother or my great-aunt had just wanted to get us out of the house? I don't know that my grandfather would have done something just because his sister, if she was his sister, asked him to, though between our first Thanksgiving at my great-aunt's house and our second Thanksgiving at my great-aunt's house, her husband died, and my grandfather spent most of our second visit sitting silently in my great-uncle's chair in the living room, trying, I understood even then, to meet my great-aunt's pain. The rest of the time, he was somewhere outside my memory, or near me, making a hole in my memory.

(My great-aunt was a painter, too. In our house, in the living room, hung a painting of a cat my great-aunt had painted—a white and gold Persian kitten, its thick hair painted in violent, straight lines, as if its hair were standing on end, its expression placid, curious, like a kitten in a cat poster, but its hair standing on end as if it were terrified of something outside the picture, something standing wherever the person looking at the picture was standing, its fear electrifying its body but not its face.)

My grandfather crossed the Piggly Wiggly parking lot carrying something red, and if it was a can its metal edges might have caught the high, cold sunlight and the cold sunlight reflected by the asphalt below him. I crossed the parking lot not watching where we were going but watching my grandfather, who was himself where we were going. Not long after my grandparents kidnapped me—I must have been three still, could I have been four?—my grandfather trained me to clap and shout whenever I saw a woman's exposed breasts, which happened most often in movie theaters, since my grandfather sometimes took me to the near-pornographic sex comedies he enjoyed. Nobody at the theaters ever stopped him; my grandmother never stopped him. The only story he enjoyed telling his friends about me—and after his friends had heard it too many times, the only story about me he told repeatedly at home—was a story about one such incident. When he told the story he would say it happened when I was two, but I know now I couldn't have been two—I stood in my seat and clapped and shouted so loudly my grandfather had to carry me out of the theater. When he told the story he never hit me.

The Dance

M ost of the day was gone. Almost a year had passed since my grandparents and I had last visited my great-aunt for Thanksgiving, but we wouldn't be visiting her this year. It was maybe three or four in the afternoon, but late autumn, a Saturday in late autumn, even on Saturdays in late autumn the day ends early. I was wearing a vest, a black vest that was a puffy jacket with the sleeves zipped off, a look I was appraising before the dance, my first dance. I had approved the look in the bathroom mirror and was now moving in it, imagining how I looked moving in the look, how good I looked, a bright white button-up shirt, black slacks, joy will take your mind from you, endanger you, how good I looked, the appraisal having quickly, imperceptibly become an announce-ment of the beauty I so infrequently, almost never, never before now, the beauty I had never before thought I had, the shadows inside me darkening my skin, shadows not even good for what shadows are good for, to hide in, my father a shadow appearing lately in my mind—I was eleven and I had begun to think, to

82

wonder about my father—my grandparents bright, not shadowed inside, the worst of them, the worst things they did and said, not as dark as the best of me. But now my beauty had been announced to me, the bright white shirt brightening my chest beneath the black vest, brightening my arms, joy took my mind and I danced, thrusting my head forward and pulling it back repeatedly like the white women in the "Walk Like an Egyptian" video, I danced as I passed from the graying daylight in the backyard, through the big glass door I had slid open dancing, into the shadowy living room, having taken the look into daylight that had not seemed gray until I began to leave it. My grandfather in his easy chair looked at me with disgust on his face and said, "You don't want to look like *them*, do you," *them* meaning not the women in the video but *niggers*. He could say *them* that way, and he had raised me to hear him when he said *them* that way. I stopped dancing. I walked to my room and took off the vest. I stopped dancing and waited for the dance.

Shame

My grandfather went to college at Oregon State University in Corvallis in the late 1950s or early 1960s. On weekends, he would drive almost fifty miles south to the University of Oregon in Eugene to ambush and beat up men he thought were gay. My grandfather never once told a story he was ashamed of.

Once, my grandmother casually mentioned that my grandfather used to ambush and beat up black men, too. The last story my grandfather ever told me was a story about how he had gathered a group of his friends the previous week, and they had ambushed and beaten up a black man. The black man had yelled at his girlfriend, a white woman, and my grandfather had seen, had heard. My grandfather told this story to my grandmother at the same time he told it to me. We were in the living room of the first house my grandmother and I would live in without my grandfather, our house in Beaverton, Oregon, a suburb of Portland. My grandfather was sweating, having just carried dozens of boxes into the house, not all at once, having just carried the last of dozens of boxes into the house, holding a glass of water, not a can of Coors. He had been holding a can of Coors for the fourteen years prior to this moment, but there was no Coors in my grandmother's new house, and we were all sitting on folding chairs. My grandfather would have been in his fifties when he told me this story, the last story he ever told me, though the next year, for Christmas, he sent me *The Collected Poems of Langston Hughes*, the last story he ever gave me—my grandmother had told him I had started writing poems—so he would have been in his fifties when he ambushed the black man. But the last thing I ever saw him do was cry after he said goodbye to me, words that meant goodbye, in the backyard of the house he had just helped my grandmother and me move into—the house he had settled for us so we could never see him again. He turned away from me and I heard him sobbing as he slid open the sliding glass door and stepped through it into the first shadows he knew would eventually become familiar to me, but never to him.

Which house was my grandfather's house? After my grandmother left him and she and I moved to Beaverton, I don't know where he went. Until just now, I had thought he moved to Arizona—I had thought he stepped from the first house my grandmother and I would live in without him, and instead of returning to California, to the last house we all lived in together, drove to Arizona, to Phoenix, I think, in I just realized I don't remember the last car I must have ridden in with him, what kind of car it was. But I know my life continued after him, like a plant growing alone in a hole the size of a house. Here I am in my life, in the middle of it, but I have buried so many memories of my life with my grandfather that my life is like a plant grown in a house-sized hole, a void, a plant yanked from the dirt and boxed, no part of the plant touching dirt now, beneath glass, the plant not touched by rain. Living with blocked memories isn't like being a rootless plant, it's like being a plant with roots that don't touch anything.

But I know my grandfather eventually moved to Arizona, to Phoenix, I think. I know because my mother stayed in contact with him. She told me his response to the news that my first child had been born was "Does she look like a nigger?" I know because my mother stayed in contact with him.

Whose child was my mother? Shouldn't she have been mine?

My grandfather eventually moved to Arizona. Eventually my grandfather met a woman there who had a thirteen-year-old son, somebody told me he was thirteen, and married her. He would have been in his fifties still. He was muscular still and good-looking still—when he was younger, he had looked like George Clooney, George Clooney with a mustache, though George Clooney wasn't a famous reference point for handsomeness when my grandfather was younger, but was instead a child—but my grandfather was shorter than he wanted to be, still, five foot eight. Though he had started working out when we lived in Round Rock, the frequency of his weightlifting sessions increased after we moved to California, when he was in his late forties. I know he never had a set of weights in the garage, but I remember he had a set of weights in the garage. After my grandmother and I left him, the house in California, the last house we all lived in together, became the first house he lived in alone since he was in his twenties. So it was never his house, not in my mind, because I couldn't imagine him alone in it, no matter how desperate I was to get away from him when I was a teenager, I couldn't imagine him without us. His house was the house in Texas, the house we came to and left as a family.

I know about his life after he asked whether my first child looked like a nigger because my mother stayed in contact with him.

Never as a child did I fantasize someone would save me from my grandparents, from my grandfather especially. Instead, I was terrified I would be taken from them—though I couldn't have been consciously terrified of this at all times, if I had been how could I have functioned? Nonetheless, when I try to recall what I felt like as a child, in a general sense, what I felt like as a child on an ordinary day, though ordinary days are the most difficult days to remember, except, for me, those days upon which I was beaten, the beatings themselves for me so far almost impossible to remember, easy to say I was hit so hard I was knocked out of my own mind, my own memory, but the truth is I don't know how hard I was hit, except I know at least once, when I was thirteen or fourteen, my grandfather hit me so hard and with such anger my grandmother thought he would kill me, otherwise not even the luxury of familiarity with my own pain, even with regard to the beating during which my grandmother thought my grandfather would kill me, the memory is secondhand, a memory of a conversation five years after the fact, and the recollection of the beating seemed to cause the person who told me about it, my grandmother, no pain. Though ordinary days are the most difficult days to remember, when I try to recall what I felt like as a child, I recall feeling terrified I would be taken from my grandparents, not even a hint of desire to stay with them, but a great, acrid fear of being taken from them.

Whenever she visited me—my grandparents, too, my mother visited my grandparents, her parents, too, but I didn't think of her visits that way—whenever she and I were alone, my mother would insist I could leave my grandparents and live with her whenever I wanted, all I needed to do was tell her I wanted to live with her. Whenever she visited, my mother would ask me whether I wanted to live with her. The anguish I felt whenever my mother asked me whether I wanted to live with her is one of the few specific instances of pain I remember from my childhood. I didn't want to live with her because she wasn't my mother—my grandmother was—but because she was my mother, I didn't want to tell her I didn't want to live with her. Usually, rather than saying no, I looked down at the floor of her car, she usually asked while we were alone together in her car, and stared until she changed the subject. As a child, I often wished my mother would stop offering to take me from my grandparents, who had beaten her (my grandfather) and allowed her to be beaten (my grandmother) throughout her childhood—not *save* me, take me; she never asked me if my grandfather was beating me. But what anguish would I have felt if she had stopped offering? Would I have hated her like I hated my father? who, as I understood from my grandparents, didn't want even the opportunity to save me?

MY MOTHER THE ECLIPSE

By the time I really got to know her, my mother was conspicuously an adult—just as I, a few years before, when I was twenty-one, had conspicuously been an adult, and had worn ties and carried a soft leather briefcase with faux-antique brass buckles even though I didn't have a job. But my mother had a job; she worked at a bank. She closed home loans. At this point in her life, she was the most glamorous person in my family. My mother had long, light brown hair, an oval face, freckles, and a small nose, and she seemed always to be wearing the same sunglasses women twenty years younger than her were wearing. But she was also the only person in my family who didn't resemble a famous person—my grandmother looked like Elizabeth Taylor, my grandfather looked like George Clooney, and, because I was black, I looked like Michael Jackson, whom I in no way, other than our mutual blackness, actually resembled.

For most of my childhood, my mother didn't live in the same city I lived in, but instead in a city an hour or so away, as if she were an army intending to siege a walled city, shifting from position to position, trying to determine the best part of the wall to attack, but never approaching closely enough to ignite the conflict. On days when I had been told she would be visiting, I would watch at a window like an inhabitant of a sieged city watching for the rescue I had been told would be coming.

For a few years, when I was in my mid-to-late-twenties and my mother was in her early-to-mid-forties, she owned a home, and had paid off years of credit card debt, and could buy a new car when she felt like buying a new car—a new *sports car*, even. Yes, a Mitsubishi Eclipse, but the sleekest, most menacing Mitsubishi Eclipse I had ever seen, black. I was with her when she singled it out, and it looked so sleek I was sure I wouldn't be allowed to sit in it. But then I sat in it, shotgun, and my mother drove it off the lot and down the wide road while the salesman leaned forward uncomfortably from the back seat and said only as much as necessary to maintain the sale. I had never seen my mother wield such adult money before. I felt both more a part of, more *in*, the world, and as if I were floating outside my body. She had gone to the lot to buy a PT Cruiser.

The house my mother owned when she bought the Eclipse—the only house she ever owned, as far as I know—was about the size of the first house my grandfather had lived in, the house in Meeker, but a little bigger. The house in Meeker was choked by trees; my mother's house, even though it was in Portland, was unobstructed on all sides, though there were trees in the backyard, and raccoons, my mother said, lived in the trees, among them, not inside them.

Before I was kidnapped by my grandparents, I had lived sometimes with my mother, sometimes with my father—the day I was kidnapped I was either visiting or living with my father, he had just bought me a Big Wheel or a tricycle or a bicycle, but I was only three years old, though my grandparents would later tell me again and again I had been eighteen months old when they took me to Texas, and whenever they told me I had been eighteen months old when they took me they also told me my father hadn't wanted me, but probably it was a Big Wheel or a tricycle, not a bicycle, because I was only three years old, and just after they kidnapped me my grandparents bought me a Big Wheel, and then later another one, one I had wanted ferociously, at the time I think it was the only thing I wanted, the first thing I remember wanting, a bigger Big Wheel than the one my grandparents had bought me just after kidnapping me, longer, I almost had to lie down to ride it, and though its body was black, it was named "Green Machine" after its green accents—and as I was growing up, when she would come to visit me, my mother would tell me that when I was a baby we lived in a house with raccoons in the backyard. That house must have been a rental; the house she owned when she bought the Eclipse wasn't the same house. And if raccoons lived in the backyard of the house she owned, they lived in the backyard the same way rain lives in a backyard on a rainy day.

Five Deaths

I.

I was born three months before my mother's nineteenth birthday, on September 22, 1975, at Providence St. Vincent Medical Center in Portland, Oregon, dead. According to my grandparents and my mother, either I had drowned in amniotic fluid or I had asphyxiated because the umbilical cord had gotten wrapped around my neck. For long stretches of my childhood, I thought my birth was the most interesting thing about me, and I told everyone I met the story, starting off with "Did you know I was born dead?" as if they could have known before meeting me, as if the story was bigger than I was, the way haloes in medieval paintings are bigger than heads. But the single concrete memory I have of me telling people the story when I was a child only contains a sliver of me telling people the story—the telling is at the edge of the memory, as if it were about to fall out. At the center of the memory I'm at a playground with ten or fifteen other children, climbing and leaping from a tall wooden tower into sand again and again. I'm trying to convince the other children I can't be hurt because I've been dead.

II

I was born three months before my mother's nineteenth birthday, in a hospital my father hadn't visited, or had visited, but not after I was born, or was prevented from visiting by my grandparents. No story about my life before I was old enough to remember my life was stable throughout my childhood. My grandparents told me I never met my father, that he didn't know and didn't care to know where I was, but also that a relative of his stole my Christmas presents when I was an infant, whereas my mother told me I had as an infant lived sometimes with her, sometimes with him. If my grandparents wanted to successfully kidnap me, they had to make sure I didn't know myself—that is the lifelong labor of kidnapping a child. And even now, after a lifetime of wondering about such things, my urge to know the details of my past is dampened by my fear of discovering that nothing I know about my past is true—this fear is the only constant feature, the only *true* feature, of my identity that my upbringing will allow.

A child can be raised to participate in their own disappearance for the rest of their life.

III.

I was born three months before my mother's nineteenth birthday. By the time I was born, she and my father had broken up. As a child, I was told—by my grandparents; I don't recall my mother ever talking to me about the end of her relationship with my father—as a child, I was told my father had abandoned my mother just as she was about to give birth. Sometimes, he had left her bedside while she was in labor and had never come back; sometimes, he had broken up with her a few weeks before she was due. The details of the story were less important than the hatred behind the telling—"What kind of man doesn't take care of his own family?" my grandfather would say; "He lives in Brazil with his new wife and their children—he doesn't have time to visit you," my grandmother would say—and the hatred behind the telling was less important than the hatred the telling was meant to inspire, a hatred to get me through any future times during which I might find myself inclined to look for my father, and without my grandparents around to talk me out of looking for him.

IV.

I was born three months before my mother's nineteenth birthday, nominally white. My grandmother, believing she wouldn't get another chance to save me, to *really* save me, to save me all the way down, maybe all the way down to my soul, to love me all the way down to my soul, indicated I was white on my birth certificate, my mother being in no condition to fill out forms at the time. She didn't tell me she had done this until I was thirteen, and when I asked her why, she said she had wanted me to have "all the advantages." Ever since my grandmother told me what she did to my birth certificate, whenever I've heard a white person use the word "white," no matter the context—for example, when Robert Smith sings "You were stone white. . . . You were always so lost in the dark" in "Pictures of You"—I've worried they were only using that word because they didn't like black people, me.

V.

I was born three months before my mother's nineteenth birthday, on the last day of summer, three years after my parents' first summer together.

The only family story having anything at all to do with the beginning of my life that remained consistent throughout my childhood didn't include me—the story of how my parents met. Whenever my mother told the story, she told it feverishly, almost deliriously, herself heated, it seemed, by a passion to convince me she had only ever had sex with my father once, and only in order to produce me. My parents met in the summer of 1972, at the Salem, Oregon, Kmart, now demolished, where my mother worked at the snack counter selling Icees and hot dogs and popcorn.

According to my mother, my father, flanked by two other boys who appeared in some way subservient to him, approached her slowly from an impossible distance, somehow both in and beyond the Kmart, dressed, she would say, "like Super Fly." She would have been fifteen; he was most likely seventeen or eighteen. She never told me what he ordered; she never told me what they talked about. But she did tell me that the car he had driven to the Kmart had speakers embedded in its wheel wells, so she might have gone outside with him—though that feels like too great a speculation;

maybe instead he told her about the speakers as he sipped his Icee. As a child, I was certain I had been born both fatherless and dead.

I HAVE TWO MEMORIES from the years I lived sometimes with my mother, sometimes with my father. In one, I'm with my mother in a grocery store. We're shopping for Tab. There is nothing more to this memory, though it might be connected to the second memory, in which I hide in a gigantic shadow from a person in a furry, full-body animal costume—the animal is a person only in retrospect; at the time, I thought the animal was an animal, a monster. I am either at some sort of event for children or I am at the grocery store with my mother, shopping for Tab, and the animal is the store's mascot, and has been wandering the aisles looking for children. Either way, this tall, thin brown animal with loose-fitting, floppy skin and floppy, doglike ears is the first thing I remember fearing. It approaches me to shake my hand and I start crying, then screaming, and back into a gigantic shadow. But then my mother forces me to stand near the animal, crying, screaming, long enough to have my picture taken staring up into its eyes.

BUT I HAVE A THIRD MEMORY from the years I lived sometimes with my mother, sometimes with my father, but it's just a memory of being in a room. My mother and I are standing together in a living room, I think it's a living room, at the time I probably knew what kind of room it was, probably, if my mother had called to me, if I were in my bedroom, if I had a bedroom in the apartment or maybe house I'm remembering, if my mother had called to me, "Shane! Come to the living room," I would have known which room she meant, and I would have come to her. She and I are standing together, and we've just come home from somewhere, a store, maybe even *the* store, the store with the tall animal with the loose skin, maybe it's the day I saw the animal—maybe seeing the animal is the memory, and what I remember before seeing the animal and after seeing the animal is the memory's blast radius. If so, then the terror was a gift—maybe without the terror I would have forgotten my home.

All of the conversations I don't remember having with other children about my father must have happened before I was eleven, maybe before I was ten, before I was nine. Surely by the time I was nine, the other kids in the neighborhood knew me well enough to know who my father wasn't, surely by the time I was nine the other kids at Forest North, kids some of whom lived in the shadowy, enormous rest of the neighborhood on the other side of the bridge that marked the boundary between my corner of the neighborhood and the enormous rest, beyond which border I was forbidden to travel alone, though when I was nine, ten, surely when I was eleven and knew my grandparents had decided we would move, whenever I did travel beyond the border I felt they knew I had crossed it, my grandmother knew, how could my grandfather have known while he was far away at work? except on weekends when he knew, too, kids some of whom lived outside of the neighborhood, who might as well have lived in the sky, who lived unimaginably elsewhere, surely by the time I was nine the other kids at Forest North knew who my father wasn't, that they couldn't tease me with his absence. That my indifference wouldn't satisfy them, what looked like indifference, but in truth was constant rage undisturbed by teasing.

By the time I was eleven I had begun to wonder whether my father really had abandoned me, and if he *hadn't* abandoned me, why didn't I ever get any letters from him? And even if he *had* abandoned me, why didn't I ever get any letters from him, if he loved his other child or children enough to stay with them, wouldn't he be at least a little curious about me? I left Texas beginning to wonder why I felt I couldn't ask my grandparents such questions about my father.

But before I left, on a day in the years before I left, a school day or a day my grandfather was away on a trip, I asked my grandmother what my father's name was, and she said, "I don't know. It's either Stanley, or his first name is Stan, and his middle name is Lee." Though the room in which we stood, our living room, seemed at once to hush and fill with thunder, she told me as if she would have told me all along, all I had to do was ask, which seemed strange to me, because I had been afraid to ask, and just about the only thing I knew I could trust was my own fear. Only later did I realize her nonchalance meant she didn't think enough of the person whose firstborn she had stolen to know his name. I left Texas knowing I had my father's name in my head, though I was uncertain which of the names I had in my head was his. I left Texas uncertain I was saying my father's name whenever I said my father's name, but saying his name.

CALIFORNIA THE DEATH

The Terror of Death

When I was eleven, my grandparents and I moved from Texas to California, from Round Rock to Livermore, from the second-biggest state to the third-biggest state, so not much loss of pride, California had a bigger population anyway, the biggest, but whenever my elementary school teachers had spoken of Alaska, they had spoken of it as if it were more an idea than a place, and hardly a solid idea, like the Alamo, but instead an idea like a daydream, so Texas was practically the biggest state, the biggest state that mattered, so an immeasurable loss. I remember my California address, 5442 Bianca Way, as clearly as I remember my Texas address, 13505 Broadmeade Avenue, and my California phone number, 455-1984, as clearly as my Texas phone number, 258-9968, but I don't remember the address of the house I lived in four years ago, and I don't remember the address of the house I lived in three years before that, or the address of any house or apartment I lived in after the last house I lived in with my grandmother. When I try to imagine the addresses of the houses and apartments I lived in before my grandparents kidnapped me, I can't remember anything, of course I can't remember anything, I was three when I was kidnapped, but instead of a blank where the addresses should be, or even a vague image of a house, many images of houses appear and disappear in my mind, one house after another, maybe ten houses, in a loop in which the order of the images changes as the images recur. No house from before I was kidnapped to go back to, but the mind wants a house.

The trip from Round Rock to Livermore was impossible. I remember it happened in a blue van almost the same blue as my grandfather's rusty Ford F-150, but the van I remember was a glittering metallic blue, and my grandfather's pickup was sky blue and rust with a patch of adobe orange on the right side of the bed, and I think my grandfather bought it months or a year after we moved to Livermore, so the van would have been its own blue, no personal association, when we took the impossible trip in it. The trip was impossible because I know we didn't make the trip in a van, my grandparents and I were never once in a van together, not the kind of van I'm picturing, the Chevy van that seemed ubiquitous in the '80s and is now most often seen with a dragon airbrushed on its side in movies set in the '80s, never. But I can't picture the trip without picturing us in a van, one of them driving, my grandfather or my grandmother, but most of the time probably my grandfather— I imagine my grandfather did most of the driving because he was the sort of man who would have believed it both his duty and his right as a man to do most of the driving, and so I build a memory about the man who raised me, the man who contributed more than any other man to the making of the person I am now, I build a memory of him from knowing the sort of person he was, an unimportant memory, but who am I if my memories of the man who made me are often guesses? I'm a loop, like the circumference of the cigarette-burn-shaped scar on the back of my right hand—and a friend of mine is in the van with us, my grandparents must hope I'll have an easier time with the move if a child I know comes along and stays with us for a few days, I can't remember who now, but I want him to have been my best friend, but I think he was actually the youngest son of the family friends my grandparents saw most often when we lived in Texas, the youngest of the three brothers with whom I played in shit after the flood, I think his family helped us pack to leave.

And anyway I don't remember the trip itself. I remember the boy, the youngest of the brothers with whom I played in shit, John, who was younger than Michael, who was younger than David, I remember John and me seated facing each other, close together, happy, though John and I were never close friends in Austin, though we were close in age, but I was fascinated by Michael, whose walls were covered with posters of Boy George, and from whom, in imitation of whom, I picked up a stutter when I was eight. I remember John and me seated close together, excited, having just been told we were going to stop in San Francisco on the way to Livermore, though now that I check a map I realize it would likely have been necessary for us to drive around Livermore to get to San Francisco, and maybe I felt the excitement I remember just after my grandparents told me we would be driving to San Francisco after stopping by our new house in Livermore.

I'm sure I've seen a movie in which a character asserted it would be a blessing to remember only the happy moments of one's life, and I was happy thinking about San Francisco in the van with John, but when I was happy had I already seen my home? Is it possible to remember only the happy moments if one doesn't remember the life?

The trip was impossible. And it's impossible now to reconstruct the last few miles of the trip, to describe from memory Livermore Valley as it looked the first time I saw it. We had entered mountains and I hadn't noticed. I had no idea how high up we were until the world to the right of the van fell away and we were driving on a twisting, narrow road on the edge of a cliff, and the valley below looked to me like a landscape seen from an airplane window. My grandfather drove as if he had driven on the cliff's edge hundreds of times before, and he might have driven it a few times before, he might have visited Livermore before he decided we would move there, and I don't know when he started hiring sex workers, but he might have already had sex with one in Livermore, and as we approached Livermore Valley together for the first time, my grandfather took the curves too quickly, he seemed almost gleeful, and I could tell he knew he was scaring me, I could tell he had already passed the point beyond which even kind people no longer know how to stop doing the harmful thing they had started doing as a joke. "Slow down," my grandmother said, almost casually. "Slow down," she said again, angrily now, and as she spoke she pushed her right foot hard against the floor, as if she were pressing a brake pedal, and leaned back hard in her seat. "Slow down," she shouted, still pressing her foot against the floor and leaning back, her body almost a straight line. She looked as if she were having a seizure, her left hand gripping the left side of her seat cushion and her right hand gripping the door handle, not the silvery handle with which one opened the door, though I thought for an instant, the thought seemed to come from nowhere, for an instant I thought she might fling the door open and throw herself from the van, but the fixed blue handle with which one pulled the door closed. Her marriage to my grandfather was her fifth marriage. Her knuckles shone whitely through her skin as she gripped the handle with which one pulled the door closed.

THE TRIP FROM ROUND ROCK to Livermore was impossible, the beauty of Livermore Valley impossible to acknowledge from the road at the edge of the cliff at the edge of the valley, the beauty impossible to see, though the valley opened suddenly, like a blossom opening in a sped-up film, the van shuddered around a corner and there the valley was, the beauty of the valley unknowable in the instant of its manifestation, all I could see was how far we would have to fall to get there. We arrived in the middle of sixth grade, I was in the middle of the sixth grade, though unattached, as far as I knew, to any school. I hadn't yet seen the middle school in Livermore, East Avenue Middle School, and so I had no sense memory of it, and so it had no body I could picture, and so I was unattached to any school, and though we arrived in the middle of sixth grade, maybe during winter break, we arrived in sunlight, in warmth. As is the case with most valleys, Livermore Valley looked less impressive the closer I got to it, the beauty I couldn't acknowledge from the edge of the valley confirmed at the valley floor to have been illusory, though it might have reappeared had I returned to the valley's edge and stood on the cliff and looked down, a halo only visible from above, a reverse halo. We arrived at the house on Bianca Way, my grandfather having come down from the near-murderous near-glee that had seized him, the white light from my grandmother's knucklebones having faded and disappeared, John having perhaps never been in the van at all, and me, still terrified from the heights, even then understanding I would have to climb the heights again to leave the valley, and descend again to return. We arrived at a house on the other side of the terror of death.

We arrived at our new house, but I don't remember arriving. We arrived in winter, but I don't remember winter, and for the next three and a half years, no winter, except for a few weeks of gray, cold, drizzly fall, winter compared to any season in California, at the end of the few months I lived with my mother in Oregon. Two weeks, or a week, or a few days after we arrived, I started attending East Avenue Middle School for the spring semester of my sixth grade year. I remember my first day at East Avenue—I've carried the memory with me, unexamined but prominent, for years. I picture myself in a brown, blue, and white flannel shirt I owned in my twenties, over a T-shirt, probably white, and jeans. And I'm sitting in the front row of desks in a classroom and answering questions posed to me by other students about myself. And I even remember a specific question, "Where are you from?" And I remember my response, "San Francisco."

For years I've carried this memory with me, for years I've played it in my mind like a fragmentary film, and for years the film has stopped almost immediately after my nonsensical response. After I said "San Francisco," a sound half giggle and half coo rolled through the class, and I couldn't understand why until someone, either mockingly or helpfully, told me San Francisco was a city with a high population of gay people. But this final moment floats at the edge of the memory in a gray and otherwise featureless space, and I can't be sure whether it happened moments or hours after I said I was from San Francisco. It wasn't until I started writing down the memory that I was finally able to make sense of my response: the memory is a memory of my first day of ninth grade at Five Oaks Middle School in Beaverton, Oregon, my third school in that single academic year, and not a memory of my first day of sixth grade at East Avenue, my second school in that single academic year. My actual first day at East Avenue I don't remember at all.

THE FIRST CLEAR MEMORY I have of my time in Livermore is my terror on the cliffs during the drive into town, but I resist conceptualizing a memory of terror, however sharp, as a *clear* memory. Terror obliterates one's peripheral attentions, one's attentions to details unrelated to the source of terror, unrelated to surviving the occasion of terror, and so it can be difficult to pad a memory of terror with details that would domesticate the memory and integrate it with one's other memories, or even allow it to occupy a space alongside one's other memories as a thing like one's other memories, as part of a set. An occasion of terror is fundamentally unlike other occasions, and what makes an occasion of terror remarkable enough to be remembered also makes it seem as if it doesn't belong in one's memory; a remembered occasion of terror is a transplanted organ the body constantly tries to reject, or does reject, sometimes the body does reject it, and a hole where the memory of the original occasion of terror was or might have been is left, a space seems to be hollowed out for the memory even if the memory never occupies a space in the mind, and the hole where the memory was or might have been becomes itself an occasion of terror, but slower than the original occasion, and longer than the original occasion, boundaryless, unending, but one can turn one's attention from it. I only notice it when I look at it, terror as the background noise of undifferentiated voices in a large crowd, the thousands of conversations in a stadium, terror as the inability to isolate a voice and comprehend it, that one can be a stadium in which one's memories speak, but neither to one nor to each other, and incomprehensibly, so that the noise of one's memories is in some ways silence, but a silence of varying shades. The first actually clear memory I have of my time in Livermore is my first day of seventh grade, eight or nine months after I arrived in Livermore, an assembly on that first day during which the principal or vice principal, for a time he had played an instrument with a band I had never heard of before, but which had nonetheless briefly been a significant part of popular culture, and might even have been featured on the soundtrack to the movie *Weird Science*, a movie which was important to me when I was younger for the sentimental triumph of the nerds, the stars of the film, that occurs near the end of the movie, but nonetheless a movie I know I couldn't watch now, a movie I wouldn't want to watch now, an almost absurdly sexist movie, but even as a small child I was allowed to watch HBO and Cinemax unsupervised, even encouraged to do so, what did my grandfather want me to see, about which my grandmother, at least, ought to have cared and didn't? The principal or vice principal, try as I might I can't discover any information about him on the East Avenue Middle School website, gave a speech which featured, near the end of the speech, a scenario which his student auditors were instructed to imagine: You're newly shipwrecked in an ocean, no land in sight, and just as you realize your situation is hopeless, a fin rises from the water about twenty feet away, which at first you take to be a shark's fin, and approaches you. Your feeling of hopelessness becomes terror. But a few long seconds later you realize the fin doesn't belong to a shark, but to a dolphin! You grab the dolphin's fin and the dolphin swims you to safety. The East Avenue Middle School mascot was a dolphin. And the principal or vice principal told us he wanted us to think of East Avenue Middle School, maybe the school itself, maybe the faculty and staff of the school, maybe the faculty, staff, and students, all together, as a dolphin that would lead us to safety if ever we found ourselves in trouble. I imagine he concluded the speech with a phrase along the lines of "Because dolphins watch out for each other," but I don't remember what he actually said at the end of the speech. What I remember about the end of the speech was thinking the shipwreck scenario was offensively ridiculous, the end of the speech in my memory isn't the actual words of the end of the speech, but is instead how I felt about the rhetorical high point of the speech, that I felt insulted, even sickened by it, but the end of the speech in my memory is also the rueful, glancing thought that I was, yes, more likely to be rescued by a dolphin than by anybody I knew.

The hills surrounding Livermore, were they hills or were they mountains? from the house they looked like hills, their slopes gentle enough that the cows I often saw standing on their slopes looked perfectly vertical, and over the years we lived in Livermore my grandfather's favorite joke became—but it wasn't a joke, really, but an observation he enjoyed making at the utterance of which anyone in the car with him, because we couldn't see the cows from our house, nor from our neighborhood, but only from our car, miles from home, at the utterance of the observation we were meant to smile, and maybe even chuckle—but it wasn't a joke, really, but whenever we drove past a cow standing on the slope of a hill, my grandfather would say the cow could stand up straight because the legs on one side of her body were shorter than the legs on the other side of her body, and though I knew he was joking, I couldn't understand how the cows stood up straight, and now I can't shake his explanation, it has become a distorting lens through which I view its own possibility, its own absurdity, and I am incapable of recognizing it as *completely* absurd, but only partially so, provisionally so; but the most distant hills must have been mountains, I had been driven along the edges of their high cliffs. The hills surrounding

Livermore, those nearest to our house, were speckled with white windmills, like hundreds of white headstones, crosses, the upper parts of which rotated where the limbs intersected. But the hills surrounding Livermore, those farther from our house, not the most distant hills, but the hills behind the buildings on East Avenue, were green with vineyards, I saw them most often in the mornings on my way to school, the hills were green with vineyards and golden light slipping from the grape leaves, each leaf somehow visible from miles away. The dirt and scrub beneath the windmills on the hills nearest to our house looked golden, too, but it was a static gold, a dead gold, above which crosses churned.

Livermore was a flat city with hills. Livermore was a town, not a city, population approximately 50,000 when I lived there, it seemed embarrassingly small to me, though I had previously lived in a smaller town, population between 12,740 (year: 1980) and 30,923 (year: 1990) when I left in 1986—I couldn't find census data for 1986. I had always thought of myself as *practically* living in Austin, I had lived at the edge of Round Rock, close to the edge of Austin, and too far from either city/town center to derive a real understanding of the size of the city/town therefrom, though every so often I was driven past, and sometimes even into, downtown Austin, and I knew it was big and full of tall buildings. Downtown Livermore was not full of tall buildings, and seemed to me embarrassingly small, though with regard to the disapproval of whom I felt embarrassed I can't say, probably the disapproval of my own sense of who I thought I was supposed to be. At the time, *who* I thought I was supposed to be was almost completely an expression of *where* I thought I was supposed to be. But isn't that a large part of what it is to be a kidnapped child, to be an expression of where and with whom one is?

My first clear memory of my time in Livermore is my memory of the speech of the principal or vice principal—whoever was sitting next to me on the bleachers whispered that the principal or vice principal had played an instrument with, though not permanently in, an actual band for a time, with music videos on MTV and everything, maybe the saxophone—but before the first day of seventh grade and that speech, I remember, but not clearly, riding a BMX bicycle home from a small shopping center, a medium-sized grocery store and two or three smaller satellite stores, but maybe four or five, because I also remember, along with the two or three smaller satellite stores, a Round Table Pizza, where I played *Double Dragon* for the first time, vaguely aware that the game was a cultural phenomenon, and the Round Table Pizza was attached to a store I never visited, and both occupied a space in the parking lot unattached from the two or three other smaller satellite stores. Eventually, I would learn a shorter, more involved route home through neighborhoods I've now almost completely forgotten, except I remember one house, close to the shopping center, with the street number 666. The house was tan with brown accents, the blinds were always drawn, and I never once saw a car in the driveway, nor any other sign of life in or about the house, but the lawn was kept short, though in my memory I picture it a green from which the greenness is evacuating, and flecked with tan patches. I always hurried past that house. But on the day I'm remembering I had yet to learn of its existence.

On the day I'm remembering I had just begun riding my bike

home the long way, down East Avenue, from the Big T, the grocery store in relation to which the satellite stores were fixed in their orbits. Though I'm not at all certain I'm recalling the geography of the area correctly, not far from the Big T, in my memory right next to it, was a BMX track I hadn't noticed before. I had never seen a BMX track in real life, only on television, and at first I felt unable to take the sight in, so glorious did the track appear to me. As I was attempting to comprehend what I was looking at, I began to realize that, even though the track was accessible—it wasn't surrounded by a fence, nor was it in use—I wouldn't be able to take full advantage of it because I had no aptitude for riding bicycles except in the most basic way. I could bunny hop, but I couldn't get more than a few inches off the ground; I had pegs on the rear axle of my bike, but I didn't know what to do with them—I had them because I had seen other children with pegs on their bikes. Nonetheless, I had to try the track.

My bike had pegs on its rear axle, and maybe on its front axle, too, I'm not sure, but I know I at least once or twice stood on the pegs on the rear axle while I was riding, that was the extent of the trick, no wheelie, though popping a wheelie would have made sense, and eventually, in imitation of Derek, my first friend in Livermore, who lived two houses away from me and who for a time, entirely because he lived so close, was my best friend, though we belonged to two different social groups—he was a stoner, which title didn't actually refer to drug use (or, insofar as it *did* refer to drug use, seemed only to indicate that such children would be likely to use drugs eventually—indeed, they might even use drugs now, were they given the chance, but for the moment they were drug-free, and any future drug use would merely be interest owed on their current borrowed fearsomeness), but primarily to an inclination toward hair metal, denim jackets, and high-top Reeboks, and I was a nothing, a member of no group—eventually I became good enough at wheelies on the chrome Diamond Back mountain bike my grandmother hadn't, on the day I tried the BMX track, yet bought for me that I could maintain a wheelie for a long suburban block, how strange it is, now that I think about it, to lose control of a wheelie after maintaining it for so long, after a few feet, maybe ten, isn't the wheelie locked in? Haven't the rider and the bicycle found an equilibrium? How can it be, even a bit of joyous, childish showing off, a struggle the whole way? I'm not sure whether I had pegs on the front axle, but I do know I had large, white plastic discs affixed to my wheels, one on each side of both wheels, covering my spokes. These discs were meant to make my bike more aerodynamic; they only made it heavier. I thought they looked cool. And it wasn't until I heard at least one disc rattle loose as I landed my first, puny jump on the BMX track—I had imagined the dirt ramp would launch me into the sky without requiring any effort from me, partly because I would be rolling so fast when I hit the ramp, thanks to my aerodynamic wheels—that I realized the discs were worse than useless, the beautiful white discs, weighing me down when I tried to jump, throwing me off-balance as I rounded the curved wall, pedaling as hard as I could now, desperate to get off the ground when I hit the second, bigger ramp ahead.

Livermore was a flat town with hills. Livermore was a town in which one imagined one would be launched into the sky by the ramp-like hill one saw in the distance only to discover one had to use all one's strength just to barely reach the top, and then it was a relief to roll down the other side, it was a relief to allow oneself to be pulled down, it was a relief to feel for a moment that, having already worked so hard to reach failure, one didn't have to keep working to keep failing. I achieved the summit of the second, bigger ramp puffing, dragging my rattling, heavy bike, though I was mounted on it still, pedaling it still, far enough from home that I realized the ride home on my rattling, heavy bike would be almost intolerable, one's sense that the hill goes all the way down to the bottom is illusory, how old do you have to be to know? eventually one has to start working again to keep failing. But isn't that a large part of what it is to be a kidnapped child, eventually you have to start hiding to stay lost?

D erek lived two houses away from me, two or three houses. I might have met Derek the day I arrived in Livermore. By the time the principal or vice principal gave the speech during which I realized I could with more confidence rely upon the goodwill of wild animals than the goodwill of any people I knew, eight or nine months after I arrived in Livermore, Derek and I were friends, had been friends, and were perhaps almost not friends anymore, I don't remember he and I ever interacting with each other at school, though I do remember an awareness that he and I *couldn't* interact with each other at school because he was a stoner and I was a nothing.

Derek and I bonded over nothing. Our proximity, one or two houses apart, bonded us. Derek had interests: he liked music, mostly metal, mostly power metal, though he did have a poster of Run-DMC and the Beastie Boys posing together on his wall, I remember feeling shocked to see the black men and white men together, feeling the black men were validating the music of the white men—I had assumed, not knowing anything about hip-hop or music in general, but knowing who Run-DMC and the Beastie Boys were, it was 1987, that Run-DMC would hate the Beastie

Boys, that Run-DMC would feel the Beastie Boys had stolen something from them, and maybe the poster existed to counter such assumptions—he liked lifting weights, he had muscular arms, especially for a child, and a few dumbbells were pushed against the wall near his bed; and he had a mullet, which even in 1987 qualified as an interest. He was about my height, but muscular and slightly taller, his two front teeth were prominent, like mine were, but his were slightly more so, though otherwise he looked like Brad Pitt, though Brad Pitt wasn't a presence in popular culture when Derek and I were friends, and I only realized the resemblance years later, his hair was blond, and his skin was pale white, he had the kind of white skin that looks pale on purpose, as if its bearer stayed out of the sun to maintain its whiteness, though Derek was as active outside as I was, maybe more so. I had no interests except I didn't want to feel alone.

SINCE WE DIDN'T MEET at school, since we couldn't talk to each other at school, Derek and I must have met in our neighborhood. The neighborhood in which I had lived in Round Rock had seemed big to me, almost incomprehensibly big, while I lived there, though eventually I was old enough, and strong enough, to ride my bike from one end of the neighborhood to the other—surely I would have conceptualized my ability to do so as an expression of strength, I was a young boy and had few, almost no, friends, rather than as a privilege afforded to me because of my age. My grandparents, anyway, wouldn't have known I had ridden to the far end of the neighborhood, why would I have told them? and I had just become interested in girls, anyway, and had begun conceptualizing most of my actions as expressions of an attractive degree of bodily competence. Once, on my way back home from riding to the far end of my neighborhood, riding my bike with no hands, I had just learned how to ride a bike with no hands, I crossed back and forth in front of a house in which, I knew, a girl from my school lived, back and forth, maybe four or five times, hoping she would see me and recognize my bodily competence, though her house was set so far back from the road I couldn't see myself reflected in its large, dark windows as I rode back and forth in front of it—but the neighborhood in which I lived in Livermore was bigger, more diffuse, seemingly a series of connected zones, in some of which the houses were years, maybe a decade, newer and less individualized than in others. Derek and I lived in the newest corner of the neighborhood, where the houses looked as if they had been hurriedly stamped into place by an enormous machine. Our backyards stopped at a tan stucco wall, six or seven feet tall, that stretched the length of our zone, and behind the wall was a long and usually not busy road, though apparently it had been designed to be busy, it was featureless, or almost featureless, in a way that suggested it was meant to be driven on by people who would wish they could drive on it faster than they would drive on it, and behind the road was a stretch of wasteland, scrub and nothing, dry dirt, as long as the wall but only about half a suburban block wide, and behind the wasteland were train tracks, on the other side of which was a large industrial area, mostly warehouses, but domesticated warehouses, not a part of the neighborhood, but painted almost the same tan as the stucco wall.

Derek and I were the only children our age on our long street, and so the only children on our street who attended East Avenue Middle School, though at the far end of the street, invisible from where we lived—my house stood two or three houses in from the corner at which the street began, or the corner I thought of as the beginning of the street, though the street of course ended some-where, too, and maybe the people who lived at the end thought of the end as the beginning, and thought of me, though I'm sure they never thought of me in particular, maybe they thought of whoever lived where I lived as living at the end of the street, I lived, after all, in the most recently developed part of the street, and in so many contexts the newest thing is closest to the end—at the invisible far end of the street lived the East Avenue shop teacher, Mr. Dennis, though the street was so long I didn't know he lived there until the Halloween of my eighth-grade year, and so my one memory of Mr. Dennis outside of school is of him standing in the doorway of his house at night, the interior behind him, beyond the nimbus of light cast by the porch light, dark except for a bluish light flickering in a room a few feet behind him and to the left. At Mr. Dennis's end, there was a ninety-degree bend in the street—no stop sign, just a sharp corner—and so it seemed both possible and impossible that the street after the bend was the same street, and I can't remember whether there was a sign on the corner indicating that the street after the bend had a different name, though the houses after the bend were older, and after the bend the feeling of the neighborhood changed. Except for two trips out of California—or maybe they were a single, long trip—Derek and I never, that I can remember, left our end of the street together.

But Derek had a skateboard. I almost wrote, "But Derek skated," and he did skate, and maybe as committedly as I would eventually skate—he was certainly, during the years, or was it only months, he and I skated together, always a more powerful skater than me—but there was more to his life than skating, and I never got the sense that skating was at the center of his life, that it was the thing for which every other thing in his life had to make space. And, eventually, Derek quit skating, and that fact came to seem the one insurmountable obstacle between us. But Derek had a skateboard before I had a skateboard, though I can't remember what kind of skateboard he had. Seeing Derek's skateboard for the first time was like hearing a foreign language for the first time—I had no context for what I was seeing, other than an ordinary awareness of what a skateboard was; I couldn't connect the graphics featured on the underside of the skateboard to any specific skateboard manufacturer, and so couldn't derive any meaning from the image that would take me beyond the image itself, just as a foreign language heard for the first time strikes one as sounds among which one has difficulty making distinctions, though one yearns to make distinctions, though one perhaps feels it is necessary to one's happiness and even one's survival to make distinctions. When I try to picture Derek's board now, I see a mid-'80s Vision board, the kind with the word "VISION" set at an angle near the center of the deck, just above which is a neon whirlpool made of squares, not circles, swirls—neon green. But, because I am now fluent in the language of mid-'80s skateboard graphics, I feel it's unlikely Derek had that particular board, as Vision was perhaps the least metal of the major skateboard companies at the time. But maybe he was given the board by someone who had tired of it, or maybe he had purchased it secondhand? I remember seeing Derek's board for the first time—maybe a few months after we became friends, and so maybe in the summer of 1987—in his garage, his mother's garage, Derek and his mother lived in their house alone, her house, the big garage door was open. I hadn't known Derek could skate, and I don't remember what precipitated his demonstration, but in his garage he showed me the board and then showed me he could spin two complete 360-degree rotations in a row on it, which looked gorgeous to me, impossible, a whirlwind configured as a boy, rising from the rear wheels of the board and widening at his extended arms, and all at once I felt it was necessary to my happiness and even my survival that I learn to do the same thing.

LATER THAT YEAR, I'm almost sure it happened later that year, on Christmas, someone, probably my grandmother, gave me a red plastic Variflex skateboard, and soon thereafter, the same morning, was it even an hour later? I fell skateboarding for the first time since I almost certainly fell off the fiberglass skateboard I rode as a small child in Round Rock. But did I ever fall skateboarding in Round Rock? On the one hand, I must have—everybody falls, even the best skateboarders, most often when they're starting out and figuring out how to ride, and again when they're at their best and attempting especially difficult tricks. In Round Rock, because I only skated every so often, not even once a month, I was always starting out. On the other hand, in my second season of Little League I was hit in the eye with the ball during practice, and this single injury was enough to stop me playing baseball forever, actually forever so far, and I didn't for a moment regret quitting, even though I was, by general consensus, the second-best player on my Little League team—Wally was the best player, he was built like a child-sized Babe Ruth and hit like a child-sized Babe Ruth—and genuinely enjoyed playing, I enjoyed my grandfather's obvious pride in my ability. The lie that the coach of my Little League team won the Little League World Series the year after I quit might have originated with my grandfather, though it seems more like a lie my grandmother would tell, her job to embarrass or shame me back to masculinity, her idea of masculinity, my grandmother who married the quarterback in high school, the captain of the basketball team—she carried the early 1950s and its archetypes wherever she went the way a cloud carries the weather that is the cloud—my grandfather's job to approve my masculinity, and though the lie, which I of course believed at the time, didn't make me regret quitting, it did make me wish I had won the Little League World Series, but even so I didn't start playing again. I might have fallen from the narrow fiberglass skateboard—though surely I never attempted a single trick, though I do remember somebody, I think an older child who lived in the rental house next door and whom I have otherwise forgotten, owned a quarter pipe which I at least once attempted to skate while riding the board on my knees, more stable that way, though, paradoxically, if one does begin to lose one's balance, it's easier to fall from a kneeling position than from a standing position—I might have fallen from the narrow board, small even when I was small, and then somehow discovered the fortitude not to quit, or I might have fallen and quit, I might have gotten hurt and then let the part of me that loved to skate disappear, I might have disappeared it, I might have waited years to look for it.

Until I was thirteen I slept with the light on, the main light in my bedroom, the light in the ceiling, sometimes still wearing the clothes I had worn that day, sometimes even wearing my shoes. Most of my childhood I felt I had to be prepared to be taken from my life at any moment. But I didn't sleep with the light on so I would be ready to be taken or to escape, but because I feared I might be attacked while I slept, in some way attacked. When I was a small child I collected survival knives, large blades with hollow cylindrical handles into which were stuffed matches, a wire saw indistinguishable from a garrote except how many children have ever seen a garrote except on television or in a movie—but I immediately recognized the garrote hiding in the saw, my first thought upon extracting the saw from the knife was "Is this for killing people?" and I imagined a scenario in which I would spring from a tree's shadow and strangle an enemy soldier, a Soviet soldier, it was him or me, though in the scenario I had been hidden, the soldier hadn't known where I was, but he had been hunting me, an American—matches and a wire saw, as well as fishing line, a few fishhooks, and other survival supplies, all wrapped in a waterproof plastic bag. I bought—my grandmother bought for me, I don't recall my grandfather ever buying me anything when I was a child—several survival knives hoping to merge their varying contents, but they all contained pretty much the same things, and instead of merging many different supplies into an ultimate survival kit, I picked the best version of each item—the best garrote, for example, for the thickest neck—and combined them in the handle of my favorite knife, a knife with a dark camouflage handle in the butt of which floated a spherical compass I couldn't read, though I suspected the compass was broken, since north kept changing, though I didn't know where north was supposed to be. (My grandmother didn't learn the difference between left and right until she was in her sixties, and instead relied upon cardinal directions, which she always seemed to know wherever we lived. As a result, I couldn't tell her how to drive anywhere unless I sat in the passenger seat pointing and exclaiming, "Turn this way!" and "Now turn that way!" And, because she usually attempted to give me directions in advance, before we left the house, my grandmother couldn't tell me how to get anywhere except by saying something like, "First go north for three blocks, then turn east," etc., which I didn't understand. So she couldn't tell me how to get anywhere.)

Because I feared I might be attacked while I slept, in some way attacked, by whom, I slept with the light on until I was thirteen. But I remember going to bed when I was a young child, four, five, in a dark room, and I remember being woken by my grandmother in a dark room—I wet my bed regularly until I was five—my most impressionistic memory, a memory in which no human body seems real, instead my grandmother and I seem to be paper dolls, and the other person in the memory, a woman walking past us, behind us, seems to be a paper doll, but the shelves in front of which we're standing, my grandmother and I, are real, off-white metal shelves, upon which are stacked diapers, my grandmother is buying diapers for me, but I'm five years old, the shelves, though they're real, look as if they're situated at the end of a dim tunnel, and if so my grandmother and I also must be standing in a tunnel, but we're not, we're in an aisle in a store, and when I recall the woman passing behind us the space in which we're standing brightens, and stretches far to the right of us, and far to the left of us, but when I don't think about the woman who passed behind us, the aisle disappears to the right of us, and the aisle disappears to the left of us, and the space on either side of us darkens, and we are standing in a dim tunnel, and my grandmother is reaching toward the end of the tunnel for diapers I'm too old to wear. I remember being woken in a dark room, and I remember my grandmother directing me, her left hand clasping my right bicep, not leading me, almost pushing me, to the bathroom a few steps from my bedroom door, and I must be complaining or at least groaning because my grandmother says, "If you don't want me to wake you up, stop wetting the bed." And though I'm sure things couldn't have been so simple, I remember I stopped wetting my bed immediately after that night, as if I had been waiting for permission to stop. Whatever started me sleeping with the light on must have happened later.

When I was thirteen, not long before I moved in with my mother, I still slept with the light on. I had slept with the light on my whole life, what I thought of as my whole life, my life after I was kidnapped, starting two or so years after I was kidnapped, as if I had spent two years crawling out of a blast crater, for two years after I was kidnapped I wet my bed regularly, though I don't think I had wet my bed regularly before I was kidnapped, two years crawling. A few years after I started sleeping with the light on, maybe when I was nine or ten, I started sleeping with a fan on, too—I told myself if someone were to break into the house, if someone intended to murder me in the night, I didn't want to hear them coming; ideally, I suppose I must have thought, though I don't remember going into such detail, were someone standing beside my bed in the night, a knife raised over their head, I wouldn't wake at all, but would just be murdered without knowing I was being murdered, and then of course I would be dead and either I wouldn't know I had been murdered or I would know. I slept for eight years straight with my bedroom light on and I don't remember why I started doing so.

But I know I kept the light on not just because of my fear of being attacked in my sleep, but also in response to something I no longer remember, something about which no one told me later—something my grandmother either didn't know about or didn't talk about, who had an appetite for telling me about my wounds. But whenever I search my memory to discover the reason, not, surely, the reason in full, but perhaps its fingertip, perhaps if I looked hard I could see the color of its hair, I encounter darkness, not absence, no memory, but darkness, like the darkness maintained by those curtains that improbably keep dawn from hotel rooms, a darkness as dark as night but less natural than night, a darkness less natural than night but where a memory of night might be. I slept with a fan on so as not to hear any murderer approaching, but I slept with the light on to keep out whatever or whoever I feared might come in the dark—whatever or whoever it was, I preferred death, I preferred the murderer.

But I remember the dream.

For years, I don't remember how many years, for years I dreamed the dream, though each time I dreamed it, afterward I felt certain it hadn't been a dream, and I remember once sitting at my windowsill in sunlight and yet in the middle of the dream, how could I have been asleep, for years when I was a child I dreamed I heard footsteps approaching, heavy footsteps, though I knew they were the footsteps of a giant not because of their weight, but because of the length of the interval between them, though they shook the earth like hands shaking me awake, though they shook the earth like a hand at my throat, the final panic before losing consciousness like the earth shaking, fear itself shaking the earth. When I was a child I occasionally had standard, one-off nightmares—being chased by demons through a dark, unfamiliar building, etc.—but the dream of the giant, eventually I discovered the giant was a giant robot, the dream of the giant was the only recurring nightmare I had, and the only nightmare, besides the nightmare in which I was chased by demons through a dark, unfamiliar building, that stayed with me through the day after I dreamed it, and also for decades after I dreamed it. I thought about the dream often, usually wondering what the giant looked like, and was it coming to kill me? And I remember when I heard its footsteps as I was sitting at my windowsill in sunlight I looked toward the small hill, though it seemed enormous to me back then, at the peak of which the neighborhood ended, the neighborhood vanished at the edge of the highway that intersected Broadmeade at the peak of the hill, though the neighborhood, the houses in it, also stopped a block below the peak of the hill, the stretch of the neighborhood from that lower intersection to the peak of the hill being first a fenced backyard, then the forest in which I searched for marijuana when I was maybe nine, probably ten, then the convenience store, it was a UtoteM, the whole chain gone now, bought by Circle K in the early '80s, but it was a UtoteM still when I was small and shoplifted dozens of candy bars from it at a time, sometimes comic books, but then only one at a time, I would slip the book under my shirt, I looked toward the small hill because the giant's footsteps seemed to be coming from the field on the other side of the highway, I was wide awake, and I remember thinking, "He's found me," but who? The giant, but who? BOOM . . . BOOM . . . BOOM. But I couldn't see the hill from my window, only the neighbor's house, next to which another house, then another, then the UtoteM, I saw all these in my mind even as the earth was shaking, and I had to picture them to picture the field beyond them, through which the giant was approaching. Were you to stand on the shoulder of the highway with your back to my neighborhood, the area would appear uninhabited, and the giant would seem to approach from nowhere, but death has no native country except you.

Eventually, not long before I moved from Texas to California, I dreamed a first and last confrontation with the giant. In my dream, I was sitting at the window next to the head of my bed, opposite from my bedroom door. I dreamed I was leaning on the windowsill and gazing at the stars above my backyard. The sky was clear, the nearest peak of the rusty A-frame swing set my grandparents had bought for me when we arrived in Texas, an artifact of their early effort to buy my affection, just touching the bottom of the sky. The giant's footsteps, BOOM . . . BOOM . . . BOOM, emerged from no approach, but sounded closer than they had ever sounded before, though I couldn't see the giant right away, though his footsteps shook the house so violently at first I thought the giant meant to shake the house into the caves beneath it. (I had never seen him, but I knew, I had always known, the giant was male.) BOOM, another step, then BOOM, another, then silence—never before had the giant stopped walking toward me, the dreams had always consisted of his footsteps approaching, unvaryingly loud, I now understood, because he had been too far away for me to notice his footsteps getting louder as the giant got closer. I knew the giant was in my backyard, but I couldn't see him. I looked to the left and saw the fence between my yard and my neighbor's yard about fifteen feet away, the swing set shifting from its place on the left side of my field of vision, not in the periphery but near the boundary thereof, to my right periphery as I turned my head to the left, and as I turned my head to the left, three-quarters of the yard to the right of me, more than three-quarters, most of the yard, disappeared. I heard a creak like the sound of a gigantic metal construction in a movie beginning to tip over, though "creak" seems too small a word for a sound I've always thought of as metal screaming. I heard metal scream behind my head to the right, and turned to the right, at first I thought it was the swing set buckling, collapsing, but the scream was too loud, I turned to the right and saw a giant robot, he looked like the off-brand Gundam toys I saw whenever my grandmother took me to the flea market, but huge, sixty feet tall, the horns on his head, one on either side of his head, were flat where their points should have been, and not cylindrical but rectangular, though they tapered toward their flat peaks, his horns were bright white, his helmet dark blue, though his helmet was also his head, his eyes a metallic, opaque yellow, and his right fist, rushing toward me, a matte whitish gray, the color of a fighter jet. I leapt away from his hand into the air, just then realizing I was no longer in my bedroom, but neither were the giant and I in my backyard, but we were in a completely empty warehouse with corrugated steel walls and a corrugated steel roof, though it was taller than any warehouse, and wider than any warehouse, and, despite its great size, seemingly held up by nothing but its walls. The camera through which I had been watching the dream, which before I leapt into the air had been my eyes, was now positioned far from me, on the ground, and I saw myself hovering about fifty feet above the ground and twenty feet to the left of the giant, who was framed by light pouring in from the warehouse door, just inside of which the giant stood, and through which could be seen nothing but bright yellow light. I held an enormous blue sword the shape of He-Man's sword, and seemingly too large for even a grown man to wield, and I raised the sword effortlessly above my head as I flew toward the robot's face, his right fist now buried five feet deep in the earth, his face turning toward me.

The giant's face turned slowly, and had not completed its motion when I struck his right cheek with the sword, severing most of his jaw. I remember thinking such a wound wouldn't kill him, and from across the warehouse, through the camera that had been my eyes, I saw my shoulders jerk backward as if I meant to raise the sword again, but the sword, though I gripped it with both hands, would not be raised, but remained vertical, its tip pointed toward the floor of the warehouse, and instead seemed to leap down from my hands toward the floor, and as it fell the sword was consumed by coruscating white light from its tip to its handle as the giant was consumed by the same light from his feet to his head, as if the sword had been a part of the giant. I began to fall from the sky toward the floor, and woke falling. And I instantly knew I would never hear the giant's footsteps again. I remember thinking I ought to feel happy—the nightmares of the giant's footsteps had terrified me for years—but I didn't feel happy. I sat up, sat still for a moment, and then stood and stepped from my bed to the window at which, at the beginning of the dream, I had been watching the stars. Wind shook the leaves of the weeping willow, the absence of which, in the dream, I hadn't noticed. The swing set that had once stood behind it was gone, had been gone for years, for what seemed like many years to me, a child, maybe two years, maybe three. But the yard looked the same as it had looked the previous day and would look the next day, though the house had been sold, and the yard was now rushing away from me.

A teenager is a person who has begun to realize they are a person. I became a teenager early, during my first months in California, when I was eleven. While my peers at East Avenue were starting to think about the lives they might someday have, I could think only about the life I already had, and from which I was sure I would never recover—never as a teenager could I imagine a future for myself; by the time I was fifteen I was certain I would die when I was eighteen, because what's beyond eighteen? When I was a child, I wanted to grow up to become a baseball player; when I was a slightly older child, after I got hit in the eye with a baseball, I thought I might grow up to work at IBM because my grandfather worked there; when I was a teenager, I couldn't imagine growing up. I didn't aspire to be more than the harm done to me, I didn't want to outgrow it—my grandfather had started beating me almost immediately after my grandparents kidnapped me; the chain of beatings bound me to the kidnapping, that great wound at the beginning of my life, and before the beginning of my life, before the kidnapping, I was waiting still, unharmed, not a separate self, but my actual self, my whole self, from which fragments proliferated forward through time as me. To imagine my future life would have been to lose sight of the chain binding me to that distant self.

Being a teenager is years of struggle to overcome the shock of recognizing the existence of other people. I don't remember a single beating; I don't remember ever talking to anyone about my grandfather hitting me. But I remember my eventual best friend in Livermore, Chris, who became my best friend after Derek stopped being my best friend, saying to me once, "Your grandfather is the biggest man I've ever seen." Chris and I might have been thirteen or almost thirteen, we might have begun to invest our bodies with sad notice. My grandfather seemed always to be lifting weights in the garage, though I never saw him lifting weights—he seemed for a year, two years? starting maybe a year after we moved to California, always to be lifting weights insofar as his arms and chest seemed to be slowly attacking his button-up shirts from the inside. He had been working out for about eight years, but never before the last year or two with such frequency. And I remember sitting on the floor in the East Avenue Middle School library with my homeroom class, maybe with the entire eighth grade—I remember feeling that the end of my time at East Avenue was too near, feeling panicked, feeling that the end of my time in Livermore, also, was too near, I must have known I would be going to live with my mother soon— watching a presentation on child abuse, maybe seventh graders and sixth graders were there, too, even smaller children, but from where? I remember a sock puppet and a child's uncertain voice, a boy standing from the audience and speaking, but too close to the presenter, standing and speaking in such a way that I couldn't tell whether he was part of the presentation, I remember thinking I didn't have any visible marks, why hadn't what I had felt been branded on my skin? thinking who could I tell? what if I got taken away? the fear of being taken from my kidnappers outweighing any fear of what my kidnappers might do to me. But my kidnappers were sending me away, one of my kidnappers, my grandmother was sending me away.

When my grandmother told me the story of how it was she decided to send me to live with my mother for the end of the summer of 1989 and then for who knows how long after that, in the event only a few months into fall, but who knew beforehand, we were sitting together at breakfast in a Carrows in a Safeway parking lot in Salem, Oregon, at a table at the back of the restaurant, near a window. I was eighteen, maybe. I don't remember how the conversation started, how we got on the subject or even near it, but I remember her saying, "I thought your father would kill you."

"My grandfather," I muttered. "Why?"

"You know it's hard for me to remember he wasn't your father."

"Sure. Why did you think he would kill me?"

"He knocked you down for something smart you said, and you got right back in his face, and I thought he'd kill you."

"What are you talking about?" I asked, my voice clear now, I remember I had been looking out the window at the cars in the parking lot, and I turned to her and spoke louder—all at once, as I began to ask the question, I got the feeling I was standing beside myself, and right away I felt I needed to speak louder so I could hear.

My grandmother turned away from me and looked into the

shadowy, wood-paneled dining room, dimly lit as if to promote a feeling of intimacy but also dim, as if a few lightbulbs had burned out, the dimness intensified by the dark brown pillars and walls. We had been waiting for our food to arrive—my grandmother almost certainly had ordered a chicken-fried steak, I almost certainly had ordered a side of ham, no main dish—and now it arrived. I watched our server, a woman not much older than me, her hair the shade of brown I've always called blond pulled back in a quick ponytail, as she set down my grandmother's plate, and I said "Thank you" as she set down mine, I had to look through me standing beside myself to see her. After she left I asked again, "What are you talking about?"

"Don't you remember? This was about a week before you went to live with Denise."

Now my grandmother described the beating in more detail, though she didn't have much detail to add—her description of the beating was more a summary of beatings leading up to the beating that made her decide to save my life, as if each beating had been a plum added to a grocery store scale. None of the beatings sounded familiar to me, none activated a memory. I stood beside myself, feeling slightly nauseated, only slightly, but disappearing into my nausea.

"He used to beat you up all the time," she said.

My grandmother's description of the beating was a history of the beatings before it, starting when I was three, just after we arrived in Round Rock—I was crying for my father, and my grandfather threw me into a wall, as if he would have thrown me away, disgusted, but the house itself prevented him—each beating identified according to what I had done to deserve it. No detailed description of the beatings themselves, how he would hit me. Would he punch me in the head? the face? the chest? the stomach? Did I try to protect myself? Did I run from him? to my bedroom? out the front door? I couldn't have run out the front door, people might have seen me, children were always in a front yard playing, not Derek, two or three houses away in the direction of Mr. Dennis's house, not many clusters of children in many yards, but a single cluster in a single front yard two houses away in the other direction, at the house on the corner where Bianca Way intersected with Shelley Street, children younger than me, seven, eight, nine, were always playing in the front yard together, I couldn't have run out bleeding and crying, or just crying. But did I ever run out the front door and skate away? But I didn't keep my board by the front door, I don't remember why I thought my grandfather would take it, but I thought he would take it, I kept it in my room near the door, so if I ran with my head down through the living room and out the front door, and then skated as fast as I could away, but wouldn't he have burst through the front door after me, but the neighbors would have seen, first I had to get my board from my room, at the end of a narrow hall, and he would have cornered me, I would have slid down the wall into a ball, my head between my knees, my hands over the back of my head, as I had been taught at Forest North, get under a desk and cover your head in the event of a nuclear attack, as I had been taught at East Avenue, get under a desk and cover your head in the event of an earthquake, no desk, no desk, had the ceiling fallen the plaster might have looked like flour in my hair, a still from a food fight in a kitchen on a sitcom, where did I go? where could I have gone?

There were no detailed descriptions. But the beating toward which my grandmother stacked her list of beatings, a plum, a plum, enough to fill a child's mouth and throat and choke him, then more, a plum, another plum in the scale, the pile as heavy as the child, then more, a plum, a plum, a plum, enough to bury him, the pile at last a pyramid, more plum than boy, more the stone at the heart of a plum than boy, a pyramid of stones and flesh, the last beating in the list of beatings was maybe the last beating. Maybe in the week or so between the beating and my flight to Oregon my grandfather didn't beat me again, and maybe after I returned to California from Oregon, in the last months we lived together, he didn't beat me again. If he did, my grandmother doesn't seem to have thought he would kill me, even though, if he did beat me, I'm sure I stood up to him again. Whatever that meant. Almost certainly just standing up after he knocked me down, standing, not springing to my feet and running to my room, not crawling to my room, though I re-member once crawling away from him when I was too old to crawl—a sliver of a memory, a flash, nausea. My grandmother had watched my grandfather kill me since I was three. What she feared, what she must have feared, when I was thirteen or fourteen and stood up and stepped toward my grandfather after he knocked me down, was him killing me in an eventually public way in our living room, that eventually the neighbors and the city and her family would know, that's how far the killing of a black boy might have gone back then, not the state, not the country, still the 1980s, but far enough for her, to shame her, not to end her life but to darken it. Whatever happened in the week or so immediately after I stood up and stepped toward my grandfather—the only description I can give of which I am certain is a description of the space between us as I approached him, it was empty and looked like any empty space, my grandmother not standing in it—after that week or so passed I was sent to Portland, Oregon, on a flight out of San Francisco, still the shortest flight I've ever been on, the plane goes up, right away the plane goes back down.

Most of a kidnapping, almost all of it, happens after the child is taken. If the child is taken young enough, and by a person or persons who intend to raise the child as if the child were their own, then for months after the child is taken, with both great caution and great intensity, and then more casually for years after the first months after the child is taken, the kidnappers must work to erase the memory of the child's previous caretaker or caretakers. If there is some continuity between the child's previous situation and the child's situation after the kidnapping—if, say, one of a child's two previous caretakers continues to visit the child after the kidnapping, and assuming the caretaker who is now collaborating with the child's kidnappers is at least careful not to speak too often and too positively about the child's other previous caretaker, especially in the months immediately following the kidnapping—then the kidnappers will likely have an easier time erasing the memory of the child's previous situation than they would have if there were no continuity between the child's two situations. If one of a child's two previous caretakers continues to visit the child after the kidnapping—the child's mother, say, and let's say the other caretaker had been the child's father, from whom the child was kidnapped; let's say the child's mother had been a teenager and a high school dropout when the child was born, and was at the time of the kidnapping only twenty-one, though she might have been twenty-two. (Let's say you've just realized you don't know the time of year the child was kidnapped. Was he taken as leaves fell, or were the trees dead and bare? Or was he taken as life returned to the trees? Or, when the child was taken, had life returned so thoroughly who could think it had ever left, though the sun burned bright and hot, and the thick leaves of the tree, when you brushed them aside to get a better look at the crying toddler in the arms of the white woman, the leaves felt too hot to be alive, though fire leaps like a living thing?) Let's say the kidnappers were the parents of the mother, and though she no longer lived with them, she still thought of herself as their child before she thought of herself as an independent adult. Then the child's kidnappers will find themselves well positioned to concoct a story according to which the caretaker from whom the child was kidnapped had not been present in the child's life before the kidnapping (which in the story was not a kidnapping, but a favor the grandparents did for their daughter), and had in fact villainously abandoned not only the child but also the mother just as the child was about to be born. This story takes years to tell. This story must replace not only the child's life—let's say the child is a boy—before the kidnapping, but his life *after* the kidnapping. For the safety of everyone involved in the kidnapping, least of all the boy's safety, he must never stop telling the story. The long work of the kidnapping is turning the boy into a machine for protecting his kidnappers. The final test of the kidnapping's success is whether he protects them after he leaves them.

MY MOTHER THE CIVIC

Like a Daydream

As I got ready to go to bed at the end of my first day at her house, my new house, I remember thinking I was starting over, at thirteen thinking I was starting over, at thirteen starting a new life, as if I were thirty and by some miracle had been given a chance to put a lifetime of bad decisions behind me, a new job in a new city, as if I couldn't believe my luck, and I remember thinking part of starting over would be sleeping in the dark, and anyway my mother had told me she couldn't afford to keep the light on all night, but I don't remember thinking the reason I could finally sleep with the light off was that I was finally far from whatever or whoever had scared me into keeping it on, a new life. But Portland had always seemed like a special city to me, as if it were secretly the capital of Earth, and until I was who knows how old, older than ten, surely, maybe a teen, I thought it was the capital of Oregon, and for years after I learned it wasn't I had trouble remembering it wasn't. I had been born in Portland, and I had died in Portland, not in that order, but I had never, except for when I was an infant,

and for a little while when I was a toddler, lived in Portland—
except for however much living in a place being born dead in a
place counts.

("Wires," my grandmother said, and "wires," my mother said,
had been attached to my head, my chest, an arm, some attached,
some sticking out, wires, as if, even at my birth, to those people
who were meant to raise me and love me, from whose blood my
blood was made, as if to my mother and to my grandmother I was
something other than human, a black body in a hospital, all my
body parts the parts of a body once dead, wires, not tubes, some of
which surely *were* wires, some of which surely were tubes, whatever
coursed through the wires being something other than the fluids a
human baby might require, my mother said she fainted the first
time she saw me in the incubator, she fainted, or "I just about
fainted," she might have said, she had been too sedated to see me
immediately after I was born, from where did the wires come? Not
from her, but already the wires were a part of me.)

I must be wrong, but I don't remember seeing my mother once
while I lived in California. But my mother must have picked me up
at the airport, and she must have driven me—maybe in the Honda
Civic of which she was so proud. Whenever I closed the passenger
door, entering the car or exiting the car, she reminded me, sometimes anxiously, sometimes angrily, not to slam the door. If I
slammed the door I would warp the frame of the car, so I had to
close it gently. She must have driven me to my new home, her
house, maybe it was an apartment, it looked like a house but in a
complex of houses, all the houses merged like apartments in an
apartment complex, in Raleigh Hills, a suburb of Portland. Until

recently, maybe a few years ago, I had a photograph of me doing a backside slappy grind on the low, narrow curb in front of the house, a brace on each knee. For the trick, one approaches the obstacle, usually a curb or something about the same size as a curb, at an angle, one's back to the obstacle, one forces the trucks of one's skateboard onto the edge of the obstacle by leaning away from the obstacle as one's wheels touch the obstacle, which results in one riding up the obstacle; the motion is quick and violent, one appears to be slapping one's skateboard against the obstacle. Sometimes, when I was thirteen and fourteen and fifteen, the pain in my knees got so intense I couldn't stand.

My mother must have picked me up at the airport and driven me home, driven me to what would now and for however long be my home, was it my home before I got there? When did it become my home? When I got in my grandmother's Isuzu to be driven to the San Francisco airport? When I got on the plane? While I was in the sky? Presumably, at any moment on the way, had the technology existed, I could have teleported to my mother's house or apartment and my mother's house would have been my home. But for how long before I left my grandparents' house would that have been true? At any moment in the years between my kidnapping and the day I left my grandparents to live with my mother, had I appeared on her doorstep, my mother would have let me stay at her house, at least temporarily, but her house wouldn't have been my home, not right away. Most likely, my mother's house became my home while I was in the sky.

A parent is a person who, if you are falling from the sky, and the parent has been given sufficient warning—say you've been screaming for ten years, it's a long fall, or they received a phone call a week or so previously letting them know you would be falling in their vicinity—will catch you.

My mother picked me up at the airport and drove me home. Summer had just begun, summer almost certainly had just begun. I lived in Raleigh Hills long enough to be first surprised, then depressed, as near-constant rain arrived and settled in, as fall neared winter. This was the first depression I remember—no nearby covered spaces in which to skate, and I remember thinking it would be worth getting hit by my grandfather if going back to Livermore meant I could skate again, my stomach tightening at the thought. But as my mother and I pulled into her assigned parking space in front of my new home, surely my home by then, right in front of my mother's window, surely my home by then, though I didn't yet know which window was whose, I felt hopeful, I remember feeling hopeful, and nervous, uncertain what living with my mother would be like. She must have felt nervous, too—she had for the past ten years been living alone or with roommates her own age, once or twice living with a boyfriend, but never with anyone toward whom she owed the kinds of obligations a parent owes to a child. Even as she orbited my grandparents and me, she lived too far from my home for me to walk to her, too far from my home for me to bike to her, she never in the ten years since I was kidnapped lived in the same city as me, and for the past two years she hadn't lived in the same state. How to prepare to have a child when the child already exists, is thirteen, and has already been one's child his whole life? How to assume authority over a teenager grounded almost exclusively in spare biological fact, authority reinforced by nothing but one's previous daylong, sometimes two days in a row, occasional visits between oneself and that teenager? She had gotten a bedroom ready for me, she must have, but it's the only bedroom I've lived in since I was three that I don't remember.

However long-term memory works for other people, for me it works like a file cabinet missing its drawers, and when I want to remember something, first I have to insert a drawer representing the thing I want to remember into a space corresponding to some aspect of the thing, so that I can then pull out the drawer and examine its nonetheless usually amorphous contents. When I recall my time in Raleigh Hills, I slide a drawer labeled "Raleigh Hills" into a space about three months deep. But if I lived in Raleigh Hills the entire summer before ninth grade, and then attended Whitford Middle School long enough to make friends, a best friend—Corey, whom I met there, and when I think about it I remember us being best friends for years, we discovered alternative culture together, which shaped the rest of my life, I remember us being best friends for an eternity, Corey introduced me to shoegaze music, ecstatically, blissfully describing Ride's "Like a Daydream" in the cafeteria at Whitford Middle School, I had to hear it, and when I did I found the ecstasy and bliss exactly where he said they would be, the harmonies igniting the melody like a sunrise igniting a wheat field, and we fell in love with Winona Ryder together, and not long after we had declared our love for her to each other, Corey surprised me, we were at his house, about to go skating, Corey skated, too, he surprised me with pencil-lead-gray stickers upon which, in white type, were the words "WINONA RYDER," I hadn't known printers could do that, make stickers, and I put one on my board right away, and took the rest home later—and if I attended Whitford long enough to become popular for the first time in my life, seemingly every ninth grader knew my name on the first day of the school year, and remembered it the next day, and said it smiling, then I must have lived there for four months, at least, more likely five months. But I might have lived there only three months. I might have arrived in the middle of summer, and attended Whitford for only a month and a half. "Three months" sounds specific, but how useful is that designation when you want to remember your life? Three months beginning in June in a suburb of Portland is almost three months of sun with some days or a week of rain at the end; three months beginning in August is a month and a week of sun, and then rain, years of rain. How to know who you are if you can't be sure when and for how long you lived anywhere?

Who, except for people with the most comprehensive memories, remembers stretches of their life from thirty years ago longer than a few seconds long? I remember accidentally dropping my skateboard in about a foot of water in a ditch when I lived in Raleigh Hills—I knew my mother wouldn't be able to afford to buy me another deck for months, if at all, and so I fished it out, but the deck was ruined, waterlogged, heavy, its pop gone, but I kept skating it anyway. I remember at the end of my months in Raleigh Hills, learning, but only for an hour, and never managing to do them again in the years of skating after, frontside tailslides on a red curb in front of a Safeway ("frontside" because I had to do a frontside ollie to get my tail on the curb—rolling forward and parallel to the curb, with my toes facing the curb, I ollied into the air and rotated my skateboard ninety degrees counterclockwise, counterclockwise because I rode my board in a "regular" stance, meaning my left foot was positioned at the front of the board, whereas if I had skated in a "goofy" stance, meaning my right foot was positioned at the front of the board, a frontside ollie would have involved a clockwise rotation) with Corey in the early dark, sliding along the curb on the tail of my skateboard, recognizing I had discovered a secret about skateboarding, a recognition different from the simultaneous recognition that skateboarding had discovered a secret about me, skateboarding having discovered a limit of what I could do with my body, which was what skateboarding discovered every day, and the next day it would discover a different limit, in some ways a further limit, and again the day after that, I can still feel the sensation in my right foot, which stood on the sliding tail. And I remember I was skating a new deck when I learned frontside tailslides, how long after I had dropped my board in ditch water did this happen? I was about to leave Raleigh Hills to go back to Livermore, maybe my grandmother had sent my mother the money for the deck. I remember having a long conversation with a girl in a small park across the street from an apartment complex at the top of the hill above my house, my mother's house, our apartment, the girl mentioning that her boyfriend, Christian, would be angry if he knew she and I were talking, was this before or after I became aware that Christian hated me, that he wanted to beat me up, and would beat me up if he got the chance, he was half a foot taller than me? I don't think I had a bicycle while I lived in Raleigh Hills, but I remember riding a bicycle in the parking lot of the apartment complex across from the park, Christian's apartment complex, at the top of the hill above my house, my mother's house, our apartment, listening to "Quick as

Rainbows" by Kitchens of Distinction, which couldn't have happened since that song was released in March 1990, months after I had returned to Livermore, but maybe I rode the bicycle in the parking lot a year or so later, after I had moved to Beaverton with my grandmother, near enough to Raleigh Hills that I might have visited Raleigh Hills to see how much it had changed since I left, the gap that would have formed, to ache in the change, to ache even in the change to an area in which a boy lived who hated me, especially there, even as a teenager, barely a teenager, fourteen, I sought nostalgia.

And how do you know who you are if you can't be sure when and for how long you lived anywhere? I remember, still, Corey describing Ride's "Like a Daydream" to me in the Whitford cafeteria, even after I discovered yesterday, just after determining the release date of "Quick as Rainbows," the impossibility of the memory, that "Like a Daydream" was released in America in July 1990, the summer after I moved to Beaverton with my grandmother, and so more than half a year after Whitford. The child I've long thought I was while I was at Whitford was developing an interest in the British music scene of which Ride was a part, shoegazing, its thick walls of distorted guitars and usually quiet, melodic singing, the guitars and vocals often sounding as if they belong to different songs, for years I've assumed my interest in music in which a barely discernible melodicism is situated amidst noise, chaos, had to do with, was a reaction to, what had happened to me as a small child, that my interest in shoegazing was to some extent an expression of a wish to be healed, or at least soothed, that I was both confronting and communicating with my childhood wounds when I listened to shoegazing, but despite what I've believed, I hadn't begun that confronting and communicating with my childhood wounds via shoegazing while I lived in Raleigh Hills, I wasn't the child I've thought I was there, and I've now realized I stacked the memory of Corey introducing me to "Like a Daydream," which he did, but not at Whitford, we got back in touch after I moved to Beaverton, and it was also after Whitford that Corey printed the Winona Ryder stickers for our skateboards, I stacked the memory of Corey introducing me to "Like a Daydream," and so introducing me to Ride, a band of white musicians (Corey was white, too—all my childhood friends were white, except for a girl, Tanesha, I knew briefly in Livermore, in the months before I moved to Raleigh Hills, but when my grandparents discovered she was black they told me to stop spending time with her, and I did), I stacked the memory on top of an actual memory of Corey introducing me to a black musician while we were at Whitford together, Sir Mix-a-Lot, and his debut album, *Swass*, in particular the song "Buttermilk Biscuits (Keep on Square Dancin')," I remember Corey brought the cassette to school and we listened to it during lunch, but outside, but he might have first mentioned it to me in the cafeteria, he might have said I had to hear it, it was a funny song. I couldn't have lived in Raleigh Hills at the time I've remembered, and still remember, living there, and so I couldn't have been the child I've remembered, and still remember, myself being while I lived there.

Your relationship with yourself is retrospective in a way—in many ways, surely—your relationships with others cannot be. You express your loyalty to your friends and loved ones primarily in real time, in situations in which your loyalty is tested, and to a lesser degree retrospectively, by being loyal to your memories of them, whereas you express your loyalty to yourself primarily retrospectively—or, if not, your loyalty to your memories of yourself is at least as important as your real-time loyalty to your idea or ideas of yourself—and, since you are the only possible source of comprehensive memories of yourself, your inner self, the betrayal that is a failure or even an alteration of memory with regard to yourself is more significant than a similar failure with regard to a friend or loved one could be. No one else can betray you the way you can betray you. But for most people it's a certainty—no one else *will* betray you the way you will betray you. As for the child I was while I was at Whitford? I replaced a memory of a black man with a memory of white men in order to tell myself a story about myself, in order to recognize myself I erased my father. Who are you if you can't be sure when and for how long you lived anywhere? Who are you if you erase your life whenever you recall your life?

And I remember talking with somebody at Whitford, another student, other students, about my father. The final test of a kidnapping's success is whether the kidnapped child, a teenager now, a thirteen-year-old boy, he turns fourteen while he's away from his kidnappers, living with his mother for the first time since he was kidnapped, the final test of a kidnapping's success is whether the kidnapped child protects his kidnappers after he leaves them. And perhaps one first assumes that protecting his kidnappers means not revealing the fact of his kidnapping to anyone not involved in his kidnapping—and this assumption is, of course, correct, but if the kidnapped child must consciously choose not to reveal the fact of his kidnapping, the kidnapping has already failed. The kidnapped child must first and above all protect his kidnappers from himself—it must not occur to him to tell anyone he was kidnapped, and so it must not occur to him that he was kidnapped. If the absence of the person from whom the child was kidnapped must be explained, it's best to tell the child the person from whom he was kidnapped chose, and continues to choose, to abandon the child. My grandparents didn't teach me to hate my father to make his absence easier for me to bear. They taught me to hate my father to make his absence safe for them.

Who blames the wolf for killing to eat? Who would not blame the wolf for killing and eating the family pet?

By now, I was old enough to say I hated my father without startling the people to whom I said it. In the days immediately after I started attending Whitford, as I inexplicably became and remained popular, I had conversations with several other ninth graders in which, in response to their inquiries about my parentage, I related my hatred of my father, always offhandedly, as if hating him were a learned reflex as good as natural, a martial art one's full mastery of which isn't revealed until one is attacked. "I've never met my father. . . . Yeah, either he dumped my mom two weeks before I was born, or while she was in the hospital. . . . I hate him."

Though I didn't recognize the problem then, I realize now that my failure to reconcile the stories I was told about my father's absence preserved the story of my father's absence like a wasp in amber: a wounding thing no longer capable, when properly considered, though one still recoils when one looks at it, of wounding.

The final test of a kidnapping's success is whether the kidnapped child lives. Even if the kidnappers took the child with the intention of raising him as their own, if he lives, the kidnapping fails. If he lives, he will look.

Maybe I decided I didn't want to hate my father anymore just before I left Raleigh Hills to go back to Livermore, maybe the day before I stopped living with my mother, because a gap between the decision and what my mother told me just before I went back to Livermore would make sense. Maybe it was weeks before I left, maybe it was the morning I woke and a man I didn't recognize was sleeping on the couch in the living room. My mother hadn't come home before I went to bed the previous night, though she had called me from the bar up the road. The distance from our house to the bar was about the same as the distance from my house in Round Rock to the UtoteM at the top of the hill, and the bar was situated on the slope of a gentle hill, into which a road had been cut, and so seemed to sit upon an intermediary peak, just as the UtoteM had sat upon the peak of a hill. My mother had called me from the bar to say she wouldn't be home soon, and I should go to bed, and I went to bed, thirteen or fourteen, but terrified, I had never before slept in an empty house, and when I left my bedroom in the morning I saw a man I didn't recognize sleeping on the couch, my mother told me later he had been too drunk to make it back to his place, and maybe it was then, so soon after I had declared my hatred for my father to my fellow ninth graders at Whitford, maybe it was that morning I decided I didn't want to hate my father anymore, so maybe I didn't hate him anymore. But whether I had decided maybe I didn't hate my father the day before or weeks before, when my mother told me, crying, she had to tell me before I left, when she told me, crying, that my grandparents had taken me from my father without telling him they were taking me, she didn't use the word "kidnapped," and no fireworks exploded in my head, no alarm rang, and my feelings for my grandparents, feelings I knew weren't nearly as strong as the feelings most children seemed to have for their parents, and my grandparents weren't my grandparents but my parents, my feelings for my grandparents didn't change, but when my mother told me my grandparents had kidnapped me—she couldn't have stopped them, she was so young, and she wasn't ready to be a mom, and after they took me they told her she would never see me again if she told anyone what they had done—when she told me, I had already decided maybe I didn't hate my father anymore, but no fireworks, no alarm, maybe I didn't hate him, but I didn't know him, and my mother still wasn't ready to raise me, and when my mother told me my grandparents had kidnapped me, what she told me couldn't matter. What I knew, I couldn't know.

MY GRANDMOTHER MY
HOME, MY GRANDMOTHER
MY WITHOUT

M y grandmother left my grandfather when I was fourteen, and she and I moved from California to Oregon, where I had lived for a few months with my mother just a few months before.

My grandmother left my grandfather, and she and I moved, but we arrived at our new house in Beaverton—not far from Raleigh Hills, three miles—with my grandfather.

Our new house stood four houses deep into a cul-de-sac, and just beyond our house, the street, which had been level, curved sharply downward, our house perched as if at the edge of a cliff. We arrived in the evening; two or three boys were skateboarding in our driveway, itself so steep they rode it like a quarterpipe. I had spotted them the moment we turned into our street, and had begun bouncing in my seat, maybe in whatever car my grandfather was driving at the time, but maybe he drove a separate car and I rode in my grandmother's dark bronze, four-door Isuzu, a diesel, she had purchased it from the man who lived across the street from us in Livermore, an elderly white man named Mr. Black, everything about him was papery white, his skin, his hair, and he wore a baseball cap everywhere, the kind of baseball cap farmers wear, with a mesh back, and he stooped when he walked, and he lived alone. We arrived in twilight and parked at the curb in front of our new house like tourists arriving at a motel. I pushed open the door, my grandfather's door or my grandmother's door, and dropped my skateboard dramatically onto the sidewalk before I stepped out of the car. One of the boys said something like, "Ooh—he skates," something that sounded like curious sardonic happiness.

My whole life I had wanted to live in a two-story house, even though I disliked walking up stairs, even though at the top of stairs I always thought about throwing myself down them, even though, having overcome the thought and begun to descend the stairs, I always felt afraid I would stumble and fall down them. I hadn't seen the new house and my grandparents hadn't described it to me, and though I hadn't said anything about it, all the long drive from Livermore to Beaverton I had hoped the new house would be a two-story house. But the house at the edge of the cliff was a ranch-style house, but looked as though it had once been an accordion and had been compressed, but not so compressed that it could be latched shut—it looked as though it would be serving a purpose it wasn't built for, my grandmother and I living in it without my grandfather.

IN THE WASTES across the street from our house and down the hill slightly, in the grassy wastes there, larger than any of the lots upon which the houses in the cul-de-sac had been built, but no stretch of it so level, no stretch of it so untroubled, as to allow for the building of another house, the wastes just beyond which a loose forest of widely spaced trees grew on either side of a narrow creek, the forest in which I stood, a few months before my grandmother and I moved from Beaverton to Salem, where I had to start my life again for the third time, the fourth time if you count the three or four months I lived with my mother in Raleigh Hills, when I was thirteen and then fourteen, but that hadn't been so bad, I was consistently popular in school for the first time in my life there, though I was the same yearning, naturally unpopular person I had been before I moved there—the space around me had changed, the weather, in Raleigh Hills the days were cooler, the skies grayer, and the people, the middle schoolers, at least, ninth grade was a part of middle school in Raleigh Hills, whereas in Livermore it was a part of high school, the kids in Raleigh Hills were more introverted than the kids in Livermore, and I fit in the new space better than I had fit in previous spaces—the fifth time I had to start my life again if you also count my birth, if you consider death a position from which to start again, in the green wastes where the grass grew in patches just far enough apart from each other for the sward they made together to look sickly, the neighborhood skaters—at one time, every child who lived in the cul-de-sac had been a skater, and though a few of them had quit, two, Aaron, three years younger than me, and Mark, one year younger than me, still skated, as did another boy in the neighborhood, James, three years older than me, who lived in a smaller cul-de-sac a few blocks away—in the green wastes, the neighborhood skaters had built a half-pipe, a mini ramp, five feet high and about eight feet across, but they had built it on an incline, and so one end was lower than the other, and so the ramp couldn't be ridden. But if it had been built on level ground, the ramp would have been perfect, the ramp in the wastes across the street from our house, which itself looked as though it would be serving a purpose it wasn't built for, my grandmother and me living in it without my grandfather.

AARON, THREE YEARS younger than me, lived in a house down the hill, two houses away from mine, with his younger sister, his mother, and her boyfriend; Mark, one year younger than me, lived with his younger sister, his mother, and his stepfather in the house across the street from mine. Mark's driveway had a gentle incline, and often I would pop frontside 360 ollies or frontside bigspin heelflips in it—tricks that would first propel me slightly closer to his door, as I rotated and my board rotated, and sometimes flipped, then pull me gently away, slowly away down the gentle incline—before knocking on his front door.

A few years after I started skating—I was serious about it from the beginning; I thought I would become a professional skateboarder; I thought I had found my life—I realized I didn't know for sure how long I had been skating. I *thought* I had started on Christmas Day 1987, my second Christmas in Livermore, when I was twelve years old. Someone, probably my grandmother, had given me a red plastic Variflex skateboard, the box would have been big, maybe it was the first present I unwrapped, and after the family Christmas rituals were over, I don't remember what they were, not a single Christmas morning, but I remember I usually had to wait for someone, the same person whenever I had to wait, to wake up, but I don't remember who that person was, but there were only three people in the house, me, my grandmother, and my grandfather, and I can't imagine my grandfather caring whether I waited for him to wake up, so the person I had to wait for must have been my grandmother, but she used to wake up early, I remember her waking up early every day, five in the morning, habitually, but was that only after her Alzheimer's had settled in, after parts of her had disappeared, but so slowly I hadn't noticed, after she started hoarding I remember she would wake up early every day, at five, all the way awake, all at once, I used to wake up at four, so I noticed, as if she were late for something, as if she were running from something— after the family Christmas rituals were over, I took my new skateboard outside, which, unusually for a plastic skateboard, was almost the same size as standard wooden skateboards were at the time, it was nine inches wide by twenty-eight inches long, whereas most wooden boards were ten inches wide by thirty inches long, and I tried to ride it off the sidewalk in front of my house, to jump off the sidewalk, into the street, but when I landed in the street the cheap yellow plastic wheels at the back of the board stuck where the concrete from the sidewalk met the asphalt of the street, the concrete extended about a foot from the curb, and the asphalt was about half an inch higher than the concrete, but I had never ridden a skateboard before—except the mostly olive-green fiberglass skateboard with a Hawaiian print on it that I had ridden when I was five, palm trees and a beach and the ocean, but the board was old and the image was dirty and blurry and so looked like a landscape in a storm—and so I didn't know that half inch was dangerous, and the back wheels stuck at the half inch and the board stopped as if someone had grabbed it from behind, and I fell into the street and scraped my left knee and injured my left hip, not seriously, but I limped back into the house crying. Then whatever happened in the house happened, and a few minutes later I went back outside and rolled off the sidewalk successfully and rolled across the street.

But a few years after I started skating, I began to think I couldn't have started when I was twelve years old—twelve seemed too young—but whenever I adjusted my age in the memory to thirteen,

thirteen seemed too old. Sometimes I even thought, but only for a few moments at a time, I had started on Christmas Day 1986, when I was eleven, at the tail end of the '80s skateboarding boom, but I couldn't have, I had just arrived in Livermore on Christmas Day 1986, not on the day itself but on a day near it, or in a month near December, and I didn't start skating until after I had lived in Livermore for some months, maybe even a year, I remember showing my grandmother the skateboard I wanted to be my first skateboard, a Jeff Jones pro model, a Variflex like the red plastic board, but made of wood, at a Target in and with which I felt familiar. Though I had been blocking traumatic memories for years, the memory of my first day skating on the red Variflex was the first innocuous, even happy, despite the injury, happy as far as I can remember, I'm pretty sure this memory was the first non-traumatic memory that became permanently unstable in my mind. I would have been about fifteen when I lost my certainty about it, maybe sixteen, a child still, no Alzheimer's or anything like it consuming my brain, chewing holes into my brain, a child still.

Mark and I started skating together right away, and so we became friends right away. He was never my best friend—my best friend was Corey still, despite the time we spent apart after I left Raleigh Hills and was living again in Livermore—but Mark was a good friend, and almost as good a skater as I was, and he and I skated the same way, emphasizing power, big ollies. Mark was the only friend from Beaverton with whom I kept in touch after my grandmother and I moved to Salem, just before I turned sixteen, though I only kept in touch with him for a few months, but he and I first ollied a trash can standing up, as opposed to lying on its side, a trick I wouldn't have tried without him there, together, in the street in front of the manufactured home in the cul-de-sac of manufactured homes in Salem my grandmother and I had moved to maybe a month before.

The morning after I arrived in Beaverton, a Saturday, after I maybe took a shower but probably not, I hadn't yet started showering every day, certainly after breakfast, oatmeal? I ran across the street, knocked on Mark's door and, almost in the same instant, his mother opened it.

"Is Mark home?"

"Mark! Your friend is here!"

And Mark ran to the door, excited, he would have been thirteen, he wore glasses, he was the first skater I had ever seen who skated while wearing glasses, and he had short brown hair and pale skin, and he was about an inch shorter than me, and I said, "You wanna skate?"

And he said, "Let me get my board. Come in." And I followed him to his room and peeked in, the walls were white and bare—it was my first time in his house—while he grabbed his board, then we turned around and left, and dropped our boards on the walk in front of his front door, and rolled down the driveway, but at the end of the driveway we picked up our boards to walk down the steep hill to Aaron's house.

But Aaron couldn't come out. He had just gotten in trouble, and when he came to the door I saw his eyes were red, the living room behind him dark, it was my first time seeing it, my first time seeing Aaron in daylight. He was almost a foot shorter than me and he had long red hair, almost orange, but a human orange, not orange like a reflective vest or the inside of the fruit, the equatorial green of the fruit's skin occasionally appearing in splotches even as far north as Beaverton, and he had freckles, and his skin was paler than Mark's, and now that I think about it I don't know whether any other black people lived in the neighborhood, but a Korean American family lived around the corner, and I wondered, standing at Aaron's doorway, slightly behind Mark's right shoulder, whether Aaron's trouble had something to do with my blackness, I thought I had seen a strange look on his mother's face when she answered the door, a look like the look my grandparents had raised me to believe meant the person looking at me knew me better than I could know myself, but had I imagined that look?

Mark said, "That sucks. What happened?"

Aaron sniffed and said, "I don't want to talk about it. I can skate tomorrow."

I didn't say anything.

Mark said, "OK, tomorrow," and Mark and I said bye to Aaron and alternately pushed and walked back up the hill, pushed our boards, if we had stopped pushing and each of us had put both his feet on his board at the same time we would have started rolling backward down the hill immediately, and Aaron must have turned back into his house and pulled the door shut behind him, he might have turned right away, he might have watched us skate away.

AT THE TOP of the hill, Mark and I dropped our boards on the street, we had walked the last dozen feet or so, over the crest, and pushed again, but we didn't go anywhere, not really, but skated the curb in front of my house, ollieing toward its edge, rotating 90 degrees as we flew toward it so we would land balanced on the edge, two wheels on the sidewalk, two wheels over the edge of the curb, with our backs to the street, and from that position we tried to spin the board back to the street, landing on it as it landed on the street, and roll away—frontside ollie to axle stall to 360 frontside shuvit out, but it wasn't really a 360 shuvit, since we had already rotated 90 degrees when we ollied to axle stall, it was a 270 shuvit, but nobody called it that, nobody called the shuvit by the name that told the truth about what it was, everybody called the shuvit by the name that told the truth about what they wanted it to be, every 360 ollie I did in Mark's driveway was really a 270 ollie, I never made it all the way around, every bigspin heelflip was a 270 heelflip and I would land on my back wheels and pivot the remaining 90 degrees. Mark and I, and Aaron and I, and Mark and Aaron and I when we were all together, leapt and spun together, and when I saw their white bodies spinning I called the tricks they did by the names of the tricks they wished they had done, but also they called the tricks I did by the names of the tricks I wished I had done, as if my body were, like theirs, the beginning of wishes about to come true, as if my body spun like theirs, as if they couldn't see the difference between our bodies.

On Monday, I returned to middle school, after a few months in high school in Livermore, after a few months in middle school in Raleigh Hills, all those months in the ninth grade. I had felt joyful, I had been new but I had been popular, at Whitford, in Raleigh Hills, and I had felt miserable, I had been old and energetically disliked, at Livermore High School, and now I would finish the school year at Five Oaks Middle School in Beaverton, where I would be new again, no one again.

Five Oaks was a smallish school, I remember Five Oaks being a smallish school, not as big as Forest North, the elementary school I had attended in Round Rock it seemed twenty or so years before, but whereas Forest North was situated on the other side of a creek, a moat, I can only picture Five Oaks at the bottom of a pit.

But a pit in western Oregon, so a green pit, a golden pit, to the bottom of which several bright gray roads swirled, seeming to imitate the movements of a whirlpool down a drain, undulating and interweaving as they descended, the gold not sunlight, but swathes of wheat that couldn't have been there, though I imagine them when I picture the school—one of those paintings by Grant Wood in which the hills seem on the verge of breaking from the landscape as individual green and gold bubbles and floating away. But I might not be remembering Five Oaks correctly—it might have been situated on the rounded, almost flat peak of a gentle hill, or it might have sat in the middle of a brief green plain flanked by semi-industrial buildings on its left, shipping warehouses, on the banks on either side of the loading docks of which I would eventually skate, I remember the banks, the buildings, but I don't remember how far from Five Oaks they were, and a diffuse neighborhood on its right. Lately, and more so each day, memory seems a spell I cast on myself—some details I can check without breaking the spell, like whether I know suitable wording for the incantation, and others I can't check, like whether magic is real. If I check what Five Oaks looked like, I might stop seeing it in my memory; what little I still remember might vanish—if I want to keep my memories, I can't be sure I remember them correctly. The same is true for most people, I think, a version of the same phenomenon, though hopefully for most people the experience of it is less extreme. But maybe the experience is just as extreme, even more extreme, for other people who have suppressed their most painful memories. But also the mind seems to develop a taste for eating memories, and bites holes into those it doesn't swallow whole—I've felt the correction of a memory via photographic evidence, for example, and more than once I've felt this not as a moment of satisfaction, but as a moment of sudden hunger. My grandmother drove a swirling road down the pit to the Five Oaks visitor parking lot, parked the Isuzu, and walked me through the blue front doors and into the administrative offices through the blue double doors on the left. I sat in a plastic seat in a row of plastic seats bolted to a long steel bar; my grandmother approached the receptionist's high desk, more like a lunch counter or a bar, a quarter of a lunch counter or a bar, the rest hacked off, and told her who we were and why we were there, that it was my first day, that she was checking me in.

Sometimes, not often, when I was a child, even as old as I was my first day at Five Oaks, fourteen, still a child but too old to enjoy the greatest benefit of childhood, unselfconscious joy itself, an age at which the most significant remaining benefit of childhood has to do with whether one would be tried as an adult, sometimes, when my grandmother and I were in administrative settings, like the office at Five Oaks, I would fantasize my grandmother confessing to the receptionist that I was a kidnapped child and that she wanted to return me—I hadn't known my grandparents had kidnapped me until just before I moved from Raleigh Hills back to Livermore, but I had for as long as I could remember felt not entirely connected to them. But in the fantasy, she wasn't the kidnapper—in the fantasy, I understood she would walk free at the end—and in the fantasy, she didn't know to whom I ought to be returned, and neither did I. Sitting in the plastic chair in the row of otherwise empty plastic chairs in the administrative office at Five Oaks, I didn't know to whom I ought to be returned. My grandmother told me to stand up, that the receptionist would be taking me to the counselor's office before I started classes, and that she was going home. After my grandmother left the room, the receptionist, one arm extended toward the anonymous depths of the administrative offices, the other beckoning me, looked me in the eyes and said, "Shane"—but she said it like my name was a question, as if, even though she had just been speaking with my grandmother about me, she didn't know who I was—"come with me."

The receptionist led me to the counselor's office, a door in the farthest wall of the heart of the administrative offices, the left ventricle, next to the right, itself seemingly a different counselor's office, though at some point in my conversation with the counselor, whose name I don't remember, though I saw it on the plastic woodgrain sign on the closed door as the receptionist approached it to knock, at some point in our conversation I was given to understand that the counselor made use of the other office as well, the right ventricle, for appointments with other students, athletes, I think she said, though who is an athlete in a middle school like Five Oaks, though a different name was etched into the plastic woodgrain sign on the door of the other office, the closed door of the heart. The receptionist knocked and spoke the counselor's name, her first name, again a question, but a question the receptionist seemed more comfortable asking, and a few seconds later a smiling blond woman opened the door and, seeming to both wave and point with a gesture of her head, said, "Come on in." The receptionist turned away and I stepped into the counselor's office.

Then whatever happened in the counselor's office happened. We must have had a conversation, I was there to be talked to, a conversation between an adult and a child, we must have been talking because I remember, just before the conversation ended, the counselor, in a voice more stern than I would have thought anybody who had just met me would use to speak to me unless they had just caught me shoplifting, said, "Look me in the eyes when I'm talking to you."

And just now I tried to remember my exact response, and I couldn't, but I remembered the information my response was meant to communicate. This exchange seems to be always with me, to be always just below the surface of a pool filled with unrelated memories, any of which might surface of their own accord at any moment, most of them embarrassing, some seemingly unimportant, like this memory—I think it's unimportant, but before now I would have thought I remembered what I said in reply to the counselor's command, exactly what I said, or, if not exactly what I said, enough of what I said that it would seem to be an arm waving above the surface of the pool of memories, no other part of the body visible, but I could grab the arm and pull the body of that particular part of the memory out, the body of what I might have said, a body of possibility. Before now, before this moment, when I've just tried to remember my response to the counselor and have failed to do so, I would have thought I had access to an at least plausible version of this past self, but of course I don't remember what I was wearing that day, and of course I don't remember how my hair was cut, and I don't remember whether I had acne yet, which I seemed to have for most of my teenage years, though it only became severe when I was fifteen, a year later, so if I were shown a batch of unlabeled photographs of me as a teenager, I wouldn't be able to identify the photograph in which I was nearest to fourteen. I have no access to who I was then, except I remember I felt shocked by the counselor's tone, the angry steeliness of her command, and immediately I became aware of my eyes flitting around the room, not settling on any one thing, I don't remember a single thing I saw, maybe a beige file cabinet, maybe a blue ribbon, maybe a picture of a girl wearing an equestrian outfit and standing next to a horse. The girl might have become anyone. Probably she knows the name of the horse still, the horse is specific even if the girl no longer seems specific to the woman the girl has become, she would know if she saw the picture who she was then, probably she knows the day, herself on that day. I felt shocked, and I told the counselor I had been listening, I told her not looking people in the eyes helps me hear. Then the counselor excused me from her office, and I left.

During our conversation, the counselor must have told me where to go after our conversation ended, because, whatever that destination was, as I left her office I thought I knew how to get to where I needed to go, even though I had never been to Five Oaks before. I left the counselor's office, and retraced the steps I had taken to get to the counselor's office through the depths of the administrative offices back to the receptionist's desk, where I might have asked the receptionist for the directions the counselor had already given me, not because I hadn't been listening to the counselor as my glance flitted around her office, but because I was nervous. I stepped through the blue double doors of the administrative offices, probably just one of the double doors, probably the door on the right, into the school's entrance hall, turned left, and started walking toward the nearby end of this specific memory of my first day at Five Oaks, beyond which lay a general memory of every day I attended Five Oaks. I feel certain I started to forget Five Oaks even while I was there; whenever I recall them, my memories of Five Oaks seem to return to the front of my mind from some corner no other memories occupy, a corner from which no bridges or hallways connect, whereas my other memories seem connected to each other by tangible lacunae, tangible in the way anything in the mind ever seems tangible—in *my* mind, at least—a tangible possibility, in the way that, when one imagines the feeling of touching a doorknob, one feels the doorknob in one's hand.

From the administrative offices, I walked to my first class, which was already underway. My grandmother had thought she was getting me to school early enough to allow me, even after we checked in, as we had been instructed to do, at the administrative offices, to make it to my first class before class started, but she hadn't anticipated my visit with the counselor—even so, the parking lot, and the school itself, had seemed quiet, inactive, even though the visitors' parking lot was full, the visitors hidden somewhere, but busy, who is ever busier than a visitor, in the seemingly quiet, inactive school. The class was in a classroom on the far left side of the building—the left side from my perspective, walking to the class from the administrative offices, but the right side if one were to think of the front of the building as the building's face, the windows in the front door its eyes, its gaze toward the wall of the pit in which it was situated, or its gaze across the lowlands from the peak of the hill, surely flattened somewhat by machines years ago in order to make its position possible, upon which it was situated, or its gaze across the busy plain in the midst of which it was situated—the middle classroom in a row of three classrooms, each connected to the room next to it by a door like the doors that sometimes connect adjoining hotel rooms, though I also remember each room only had three walls, and was open to the hallway that ran alongside it, it was faster, insofar as one needn't open a door to do so, to step around the wall separating one room from the next than to pass from one room to the next through a door. I must have introduced myself to the teacher, who must have directed me toward an empty desk in the first row of desks and then introduced me to the class, at the end of which introduction the exchange between me and the rest of the class that ended with my confusion about why my new classmates were laughing occurred. All morning I had felt like I was returning to a childhood I had left, and now the feeling was confirmed, the bewilderment, the laughter.

Starting when I was eleven I gave up living my life. Every morning a refusal, every afternoon, and then sleep. Before we moved to Livermore I hadn't wanted my life to change—I hadn't wanted to leave Round Rock, my friends—and after it changed, I didn't want my life. When I was seven or eight, it occurred to me—and the notion struck me with the force of a revelation; remembering the moment now, I think it must have been the first time I felt what it now feels like to stumble across something that at least seems like an insight while writing, a glorious feeling, the body filled with light—it occurred to me that every physical sensation was a form of pain, even pleasurable sensations were warnings. When I had the thought, I was straddling a branch in the smaller of the two trees in my backyard, or climbing the tree, or descending it—I was involved with branches. At the time, the thought didn't seem sad to me, that I was in pain always—everyone was in pain always, and yet some people seemed happy, or at least the idea that some people were happy was usually imaginable. But I now realize I had begun to tell myself it was OK to be in pain always, and so, though the moment felt like a moment of acceptance,

I had begun to make it possible for me to refuse—not only harmful things, but everything. In Livermore, I began committedly refusing school, to perform at school, though I had earned my first F on a report card at the end of my last semester in Round Rock, my first semester at the first of the five schools I would attend during my middle school years. All my life in California, from age eleven to age fourteen, I had still dimly understood school was meant to make one's future life possible. But in Livermore I had been only one move away from where I wanted to be, my past life, contiguous with the only, though imaginary, future life I wanted. In Beaverton, I was two moves away, an infinite number of moves.

MY FIRST DAY at Five Oaks eventually ended—it ended weeks after it started, as all first days in some sense always end, once it had begun blurring into every other day at Five Oaks, but also a few hours, seven? after it started—and I don't remember how I got home. Probably my grandmother picked me up and drove me home, though we would have gone to a grocery store on the way, in at least one version of the possible landscapes of Five Oaks a Fred Meyer is positioned obliquely between Five Oaks and our house. But I might have walked home, I remember walking home, if not the first day, then the second, conglomerate day, at least once walking home with friends, eventually I made friends at Five Oaks and at least one of them lived on the route I would take from my house to school, Michelle, eventually I made friends at Five Oaks who were girls. Michelle was a huge fan of the band Faith No More, of whom I would have just heard, "Epic" was a hit but I couldn't get into Mike Patton's delivery, but Michelle spoke excitedly of the Chuck Mosley period, wasn't he black? For a time we were good friends, close enough to talk regularly on the phone, the simultaneously local and transient, particular and universal friendships of teenagers. Michelle was as tall as me, maybe I was five foot seven then, she had long, curly auburn hair, and dressed like an occupant of a social tier to which neither I nor most of our mutual friends had any hope of ascending, but Michelle's long love of Faith No More made her strange in the context of kids at Five Oaks, and even if I had just heard of Faith No More and couldn't get into Mike Patton's delivery, Faith No More made our friendship possible, and I bought the cassette.

But I might have biked home. I started at Five Oaks in the spring semester, and so I started in rain or rain coming, but I can't remember a single rainy day from the months I was a student there, and not from the months after, and not from the whole year after, after which, in the summer after my sophomore year at Aloha High School, my grandmother and I moved to Salem, Oregon. Still, my grandmother must have driven me home on rainy days, which must have happened often during the months I was a student at Five Oaks. I have no memories of rainy days while I was a student at Five Oaks, but I have a hint of a memory of my grandmother telling me she would drive me home on rainy days, to wait for her after school. She was free most days. She didn't have a job—she never had a job after she divorced my grandfather—but that didn't seem strange to me. We lived on my grandfather's money—$1,400 a month—plus several packets of Monopoly-money-ish food stamps a month, and a mysterious amount of savings. The trick, but it wasn't a trick, though one smiled inwardly as if it were a trick, was to spend a dollar food stamp on a five-cent candy so the cashier, grimacing as if they had just been tricked, would have to give ninety-five cents, cash, in change.

Shouldn't I remember whether my grandmother picked me up? But the memory is conditional. My grandmother might have picked me up—I remember the Isuzu pulling up to the red curb in front of the school, but then, it must be a reflex, I see myself leaning on the passenger door and talking to my grandmother through the window, probably because I've seen people do exactly that so many times in movies and on television, and the mind has to fill the holes with something, as if I were telling her, as I sometimes did at fourteen, "I don't want to leave yet, I'll skate home," but I might have walked home, though I don't remember the loneliness I surely would have felt walking home after my first day at a new school, but how many specific instances of loneliness does one remember from one's childhood, loneliness itself, not loneliness mixed with fear, or loneliness mixed with anger, not long stretches, weeks, months, of loneliness, but a few isolated minutes, a half hour, of loneliness itself? but I might have biked home, the speed compensating for the loneliness, the speed tricking me into thinking I wasn't lonely, nothing to be compensated for, any second I might bunny hop off the sidewalk, but majestically, tweaking the tail of the bike into the air, someone might see me, how a child is never convinced, no matter how often the experiment fails, that being transitorily admired, flashing brilliantly across a stranger's eye, isn't the same thing as being loved.

IT'S SOME MAGIC STOPS ME remembering my life—what else to call it? a suffocating wonder—but the magic itself occupies the space where the memories would otherwise be. The shortest route from Five Oaks to my house in Beaverton, I just checked, was too long for me to have walked, 1.7 miles, though I remember I walked that route every day, I biked it every day, but I couldn't have ridden my bike home at the end of my first day at Five Oaks since my grandmother had driven me to school and the Isuzu had a small trunk. By the end of the day, the day had already begun to blur into the next day, and every other school day in the months to come until the end of the school year, after which, after the summer, Aloha High School. I remember lifting my bike from the trunk at the beginning of the day. I remember a beginning to make sense of the end.

Eventually I made friends at Five Oaks, but that's not the right way to say it. Eventually I made friends who also attended Five Oaks, but we all, except for Michelle, lived on the cul-de-sac, and I might have become friends with them on the cul-de-sac. When I picture the cul-de-sac, Salix Place, I see children buzzing from one side of the street to the other and back again, as if they were darting across traffic, as if they were hailing taxis, I must have become friends with them there, a cul-de-sac upon which there were eleven houses. I met Tricia on Salix Place. She lived with her parents and her older brother in the house at the far corner. If you were turning onto Salix Place from Salix Terrace, onto which you had just turned from 185th Avenue, the road connecting the neighborhood to the rest of the world, the neighborhood itself circular, a large cul-de-sac from which several smaller cul-de-sacs budded, the first house in the neighborhood would be on your right, and Tricia's house would be on your left. Tricia's brother was athletic, and mostly hung out with their immediate neighbor, whose face reminded me of Mr. Dennis's face, my shop teacher at East Avenue, the same compactness, his upper lip a placeholder for the mustache he wasn't yet old enough to grow—they played basketball at the portable hoop at the edge of the street in front of Tricia's house. Tricia was almost as tall as Michelle, and so almost as tall as me, and had long, straight dark hair, was it black? and pale skin. Like Michelle, she dressed and looked as if she belonged to a social class upon which I and my other friends could only gaze from a distance, but she lived just a few houses away from me, and Mark, and Aaron, and we were all friends. For a time, Tricia and I were almost best friends—it was in her living room that I first heard "Epic," Tricia thought Mike Patton was hot—and I feel that the absence of clear memories of our friendship is as significant, maybe more significant, than any other absence, any other loss, of memories from the year and a half I lived on Salix Place, most of our friendship gone, most of my friendships with Aaron and with Mark, with Michelle, gone. Except I remember standing in a circle with our mutual friends, four or five of us, in front of Michelle's house, and someone, maybe Michelle, pointing out that the goth look I wanted, whoever said it couldn't have known how desperate I felt to achieve that look, black shirt, black trousers, black overcoat, black shoes, was ruined by my white socks, my trousers too short to cover them, me realizing then for the first time that I could buy black socks if I wanted black socks, that black socks weren't only for adults, though I didn't buy them afterward because I didn't feel old enough for them, black socks were my grandfather's socks. And I remember skating with Aaron and Mark, the three of us together at a spot, a ledge about fourteen inches high upon which a few tricks later I would break my right ankle, my second or third broken bone. I remember the trick, it was nothing, I remember it even though as I approached the ledge I hadn't committed to doing any particular trick, that would be the problem, and I ended up doing an ollie to feeble stall, I ollied up to the ledge, turning my board about forty-five degrees to the right as I rose, so that I landed with my front wheels on top of the ledge and the axle of my rear truck on the lip of the ledge, and my right foot, the foot on the tail of my board, slipped off the board and I fell, breaking my right ankle, after which Aaron and Mark pushed me home as I sat on my board, but before which, before the stall, each of us taking turns at the ledge, one at a time, flying up to it while the others watched, none of us knowing what the skater approaching the ledge was about to do, all of us knowing what the skater approaching the ledge was capable of doing, and all of us knowing the skater approaching the ledge also was capable of leaping beyond what we knew he was capable of doing to do a new, more difficult trick, the next thing could be anything.

And I remember sitting with Tricia on her living room floor, the multicolored light blazing from the "Epic" video igniting the walls and the furniture, Tricia's cheeks lit by that light, her smile lit by that light, a friendship from the middle of which, even from the moment of one's strongest feelings, one can see the end, the fiery winds in which one is carried to the end.

Almost from the moment we arrived at Salix Place my grandmother wanted to leave it, and now that I'm trying to understand what might have drawn her to Beaverton in particular, I can't think of any reason she would have chosen to move there rather than anywhere else. Her family, my family, her side of it, lived almost fifty miles away, in Salem, but after years of living thousands of miles away from them, never once visiting them, though her mother came to visit us once or twice when we lived in Texas, then years of living hundreds of miles away from them, never once visiting them, and it was during the three and a half years we lived in California that her mother died, my grandmother with the telephone receiver in her right hand, kneeling, bending low, on the floor just outside the bathroom in the bedroom she still shared with my grandfather, my grandfather both kneeling beside her and covering her with his arms and chest, after the years of thousands, then hundreds, of miles, a little under fifty miles might have seemed close enough. At the time, my mother still lived in Raleigh Hills. Again my mother and I weren't living in the same city, but since each of us lived in a suburb of Portland, we were also living in the same city. And whenever she visited, still she seemed to be visiting from hundreds of miles away. But at least once, if I remember correctly, what do I remember? I called her to ask if I could stay with her, to get away from my grandmother.

Whatever happened before the call, whatever fight, I don't remember. But my mother didn't let me stay with her, too short notice.

My grandmother didn't work while we lived in Salix Place, but also she never worked again. She had wanted to return to working in real estate, selling houses, appraising houses, or both, in Livermore, but as far as I know she didn't actually do so. Later, after we left Beaverton and moved to Salem, she set up an office in her spare bedroom, our spare bedroom, she put a large desk in the room, and a fax machine, and a computer, and a printer, and a copier, I don't know where she got the money to buy such things, and that was work, setting the office up was work, it would have been more accurate to say she never got paid to work again, but as far as I know she never had a single client.

A thing you can witness that ought to be instructive, but not a lesson you can learn, not a mistake you can avoid making yourself: by the time you realize you've left your life behind it's too late to return to your life.

Maybe a year before I moved out—I left when I was eighteen—and so five years before she started hoarding, before her office filled with furniture from nowhere, office chairs, sure, but not from her office, as if they had been poured from a truck through the window, before which her office was for a year my first daughter's bedroom, my grandmother established her final business there, trying again to sell Abbage Patch Kids. She didn't stitch new dolls, since she still had the first batch she had stitched in Round Rock, she had moved them with us from house to house to house to house, but she made new copies of the birth certificate on her copier. She figured Cabbage Patch Kids were due for a comeback, and she figured Abbage Patch Kids might spark the comeback, all she needed was to sell one doll to the right person, and that single right person would tell several further right people, and those right people would buy a few Cabbage Patch Kids, thinking surely that was what the first right person had been shouting, they would think, "Cabbage Patch Kids," surely that was the doll the first right person had been waving around excitedly, what's an abbage patch? and the subsequent craze would then consume her dolls, finally she would be rid of them—but not Fritz, the lonely, black, actual Cabbage Patch Kid, whom she had not made herself and therefore had to keep.

She even bought an ad in the Nickel Ads classifieds. But the right person never came, the right person never even called, though she did get one call, and my grandmother never sold a doll.

Forever

Each of my teenage years was years long, especially the first four, ages thirteen through sixteen. Time seems to have started speeding up while I was seventeen—I hardly remember anything that happened while I was seventeen, though I remember eighteen, I seem to remember a lot of what happened while I was eighteen, time had begun to move at what I suspect was a normal pace, or I had begun to move through time at a normal pace, is that what becoming an adult is? though I was hardly an adult. It would be more accurate to say each of my teenage years except the last two was years long—nineteen must have only been a year long, just like eighteen, but I hardly remember it, just like seventeen. A blank in your memory can represent forever, an instant, or any length of time between forever and an instant. But you haven't lived forever.

I seemed to live in Beaverton forever, but I think I only lived there a year and a half—the end of ninth grade, and the whole of my first traversal of tenth grade. (Though I had been failing classes for years by the time I first attempted tenth grade, my grandmother decided that was the year I ought to repeat, and so after we moved to Salem—a summer move, which meant I would start the school year at the beginning of the school year, which seemed like a luxury—she enrolled me in the tenth grade. Since I had skipped kindergarten or first grade, my grandmother reasoned, repeating the tenth grade would give me the chance to take classes with kids my own age, and therefore repeating the tenth grade would be a good thing. But it seemed like a step backward to me, a final erasing of any promise I might have once shown.) I skated through forever with Mark and Aaron, sometimes Corey, Corey again in my last months in Beaverton, in the weeks or months of my second summer there, but the first part of forever, the months of Five Oaks and the summer after Five Oaks, almost entirely with Mark and Aaron alone.

Across the street from our neighborhood, across the road trafficked like a highway, but it was a numbered street, 185th, was a lumberyard, I think it belonged to Parr Lumber—I remember the yard was there, but it's not there now. On weekdays, the lumberyard must have been open, it was a lumberyard but also a storefront, more accurate maybe to say a lumberyard attached to which was a building dedicated to the sale of the lumber in the yard, in my memories the building looks something like a cross between a warehouse and a barn, with a first floor—though the term "first floor" doesn't seem to correspond to the lower level of a warehouse, but what else to call it, since "lower level" suggests, even if only as a whisper at the edge of possibility, a level that might be underground—a first floor as wide and deep as a warehouse, but with an enormous Dutch gable roof, cut into which was a large, open window which couldn't have existed, and it's when I consider the large, open window, pure, solid blackness behind it, that I realize I don't remember what the building looked like, though, with regard to the image of the building in my memories, I also realize I don't know where remembering ends and inventing begins. Does inventing begin at the building's door, curiously like the front door of the manufactured home in which my grandmother and I lived after we moved from Beaverton to Salem? Does inventing begin at the perimeter of the building itself, which might have been less wide and less deep than I remember? Perhaps the building was only as big as the manufactured home in which my grandmother and I lived after we moved from Beaverton to Salem. Does inventing begin at the roof? Do I add a story to the building?

But the lumberyard closed early on weekdays, at four thirty in the afternoon, which seemed unreasonably early to me, though I didn't know what hours people who might shop at a lumberyard clearly meant to serve contractors might keep. And the lumberyard was closed on weekends. And sometimes, for a change of scenery, though the street on which we lived was in many ways superior for skating, particularly because I had waxed the curb in front of my house, making it slippery enough to easily grind and slide, or because the lumberyard's parking lot was large, empty, and undisturbed whenever the lumberyard was closed, Aaron, Mark, and I would skate in the lumberyard's parking lot, though skating in the lumberyard's parking lot really meant, at first, rolling across the lumberyard from one end to the other and back again, gazing through the chain-link fence at the stacks of lumber beyond it, the smallest of which were only a few feet high, and all of which were wide enough to skate, "to skate," with regard to the stacks of lumber, meaning only to roll across a stack lengthwise and then ollie off the end, it wouldn't have occurred to any of us to try any trick more complicated than an ollie, maybe a frontside 180 ollie, which is an ollie combined with a 180-degree turn, so that one starts out rolling forward, and ends up rolling backward. After days of skating in the parking lot that seemed like years of skating in the parking lot, one of us, I think it was Aaron, the youngest and smallest, and so the most daring of us, climbed over the chain-link fence—it was high but it wasn't topped by barbed wire or any other special deterrent, and none of us could see a security camera anywhere in the yard or attached to the building—and into the yard itself. And Mark and I followed him.

The world inside the fence seemed both larger and more constricted than the world outside the fence. Instead of immediately climbing one of the smaller stacks of lumber and thereafter ollieing off it, each of us rolled, each in a different direction, deeper into the lumberyard, each of us hoping to find something better to skate than the stacks of lumber—*I* was hoping to find something better, and can only assume Aaron and Mark were hoping to find something better, too. One develops, as a skater, a new eye for the relevant utility of objects in the world, though it would perhaps be just as true to say that, when one is a skater, objects in the world reveal their previously unseen faces to one, each thing exposes a new aspect of itself, through which its personality is seemingly expressed more fully than it was before one was a skater; when one is a skater, as one observes the world, one calls to inanimate objects in a language one didn't know before, and those objects respond in that language; though one might eventually stop skating, one never stops hearing the new voice of the curb, the new voice of the bench, the new voice of the loading dock, the new voice of the long stack of lumber, and if one does stop skating, the world fills with whispers to which one cannot respond, whispers that seem spoken in the true voices of things, though before one started skating one would have thought the true voice of the curb was a person stepping off the curb, or stepping up the curb, or accidentally brushing a tire of their car against the curb as they parked alongside it, had they ever thought of such a thing; when one is a skater, one hears the voice of the curb even when one is nowhere near the curb; when one is a skater, one considers what one might say back to the curb. Each of us rolled deeper into the yard on shiny black asphalt flecked with peach-colored slivers of wood the shape of square-cut nails.

But, none of us having discovered anything better than the stacks of lumber that had lured us over the fence in the first place— I had seen, behind the building in which sales were conducted, a device that looked like a water pump, a hand pump like the water pump in *The Miracle Worker*, but bright red and squat, and surrounded on three sides, the wall of the building protecting the fourth side, by curbs that immediately proved too sticky to skate— we converged again where we had started, beside a stack of boards about two feet high, three feet wide, and ten feet long. The stack was held together by thin metal bands, two or three thin metal bands, a band encircled the stack approximately a foot from each end, and if a third band encircled the stack, the third band encircled the stack approximately at the middle. One of us—Mark, maybe, or Aaron, maybe it was Aaron, since he hopped the fence first, or maybe me—climbed the stack, if it was Mark or me, whoever it was probably placed one hand on top of the stack and hopped up, his skateboard in his other hand, if it was Aaron, Aaron probably put both hands on top of the stack, hopped up, and asked us to hand him his board. Then whoever stood on top of the stack at one end of the stack, his board beneath one foot, his hands probably on his hips as he considered the drop, a two-foot-tall object looks taller than two feet tall when you're standing on top of it with a skateboard, pushed himself forward with the foot on the stack, probably he only pushed once, and almost immediately rolled off the end, he didn't ollie, just dropped, dropped two feet to the asphalt, and rolled slowly away, maybe he rolled four or five feet before he turned around to watch whoever would climb the stack next climb the stack and repeat exactly what he had just done. Probably the second time around we ollied off the stack, maybe the third time around one of us tried a frontside 180 ollie and the other two ollied as they had the time before. By the fourth or fifth time around each of us would have tried a frontside 180 ollie, by the sixth or seventh time around each of us would have landed a frontside 180 ollie, and the fear that we would get caught inside the fence increased in each of us as the willingness to do and watch the same two tricks again and again decreased—though one of us, Mark or I, might have tried a one-footed ollie off the stack, an ollie in the midst of which, midair, the skater kicks their front foot forward off the board. When doing a one-footed ollie, the skater looks as if they are dancing with the air, but the skater also looks as if they are fighting the air, kicking the air. One of us might have kicked the sky—or two of us, two of us might have kicked the sky, not at the same moment, sequentially, but together—as he flew off the stack of long boards inside the enormous cage on an afternoon we spent forever together.

Forevers

Forever ends. Again and again forever ends and you live past the end. Not only are forevers ending all around you even as you read this, but you yourself are constantly, if imperceptibly, moving toward the ends of what had once seemed like lifetime commitments, your interest waning, your body aging in such a way as to make difficult that trick you had for so long loved to do, eventually even standing on a skateboard will feel strange, though riding a skateboard had once seemed to you more natural than walking. Probably my grandmother had begun thinking about moving from Beaverton to Salem almost as soon as we arrived, but I didn't know we were moving until a few months before we moved. She might have told me in the middle of my sophomore year of high school, my first and only year at Aloha High School, did ninth grade at Five Oaks Middle School count as my freshman year of high school? I had spent some months of that school year as a freshman at Livermore High School. Whenever she told me we were moving, I felt numb hearing the news, but maybe it would be more accurate to say the everyday sadness I felt before I heard the news was neither altered nor interrupted by the news.

My mother visited me for an afternoon during my last year in Beaverton. At the time, my mother usually drove a muscle car, a Dodge, I think, blue, though I don't remember the model, that had been revitalized by her then boyfriend, now an ex, for more than twenty years an ex, Brett, a man shorter and quieter than his name might suggest, who wanted to adopt me, my mother had told me months before, smiling, since Brett didn't have any children, and I didn't have a father. Maybe it was Brett's car; this was years before the Eclipse. I don't remember anything about the visit except near the end of it, maybe just before she drove away, just before she vanishes from my memory of the only visit to me I remember her making while I lived in Beaverton, but she must have visited more than once, though by now she had stopped asking me whether I wanted to live with her, and she had stopped telling me I could come to live with her whenever I wanted, we had already lived together once, once since the first time she gave up living with me when I was three—just before she drove away she let me drive the car around the neighborhood, the neighborhood itself circular, a large cul-de-sac from which several smaller cul-de-sacs budded, I was fifteen, old enough for a learner's permit, and I would turn sixteen in a few weeks, didn't I want to learn to drive? I don't remember clearly where I started driving the car, whether my mother let me pull away from the waxed curb in front of my house, but she wouldn't have parked in the driveway, whether she stopped in the middle of the street in front of my house or stopped at the intersection of Salix Place and Salix Terrace, stepped from the car into the middle of the street, so little traffic in front of my house, so little traffic at the corner, and told me I could drive. She might have stopped anywhere, she might have decided she would do that bit of parenting anywhere, twelve years now since she let her parents take me from my father, how many years back then, three? since she had escaped her father, but how many years since he had last beat her? How many years would it take? How many years before she convinced herself he wouldn't do the same to me? or did she not need to be convinced? When I told her, years after she let me drive the car, that he had done the same to me, she said she had thought he wouldn't hurt me because he had always wanted a son. Maybe she spent days convincing herself to give him that gift, maybe she spent the few minutes, but maybe fifteen, twenty, she might have spent, under different circumstances, convincing herself to buy him a good-quality tie for Father's Day, how little money she had then. She might have stopped anywhere. But I remember the car parked at the top of the hill at the far end of Salix Ridge, the longish street that became Salix Place after it crossed Salix Terrace—I don't remember my mother stopping the car, opening the door, and stepping from the car, but I remember the car itself, parked at the top of the hill, growling, my mother not in the driver's seat, I must have walked in front of the car from the passenger side to the driver's side, I remember the blue hood, vibrating, and I remember my mother telling me not to worry, the car would roll to my house on its own from there, all I had to do was steer it.

Beaverton was where I stopped pretending I wanted a future. Before my grandmother and I moved to Beaverton, in the years between Round Rock and Beaverton, the three and a half years of Livermore, I had at least played the role of a child who wanted to do well at school, presumably in preparation for a future—though I hadn't done well at school, because I hadn't cared to do well at school, because no future. When my grandparents asked me why I wasn't doing well at school, I at least feigned appropriate interest in the question, and appropriate concern, and appropriate bewilderment. However, after my grandfather left my grandmother and me in Beaverton—technically, my grandmother left him, divorced him, but since he had helped us move, he left the house last (his last words to me were "Why are you so destructive?")—I stopped feigning an interest I didn't feel, a concern I didn't feel, a bewilderment I didn't feel. Whatever most teenagers feel, whatever they think, when they consider the years ahead of them, especially those years immediately ahead of them, during which they presumably expect to begin to establish independent, adult lives, or at least to begin to survey the landscapes in which they will eventually establish independent, adult lives, fifteen-year-olds, even younger teens, maybe, whatever they feel about their own futures, whatever they think about their own futures, I didn't feel the same feelings, I didn't think the same thoughts, I'm almost certain I didn't, I'm almost certain I never felt and thought in the same ways. I aggressively didn't have feelings about the future. I didn't just defend myself against such feelings, but I attacked them where they began.

Imagine a well like a well in a movie, a small hole in the ground encircled by a low stone wall, in the middle of an otherwise empty space, a well in the floor of a dark warehouse, and at the top of the well stands a hugely muscular man, he, yes, he resembles He-Man, a cartoon I didn't even like when I was a child, though it haunts me now more profoundly than any of the cartoons I liked, who watches for the shadowy creatures that attempt to emerge from the dark interior of the well, themselves exactly as dark as the dark interior of the well, and whenever one of the creatures begins to emerge, whenever a head appears above the surface of the darkness—it resembles a bubble on the surface of water, as if the darkness in the well were boiling—whenever a head appears above the surface of the darkness, this He-Man-like man punches the figure on the top of the head and the figure falls back and disappears altogether in the darkness of the well, such were my feelings about the future, I punched it in the head. And I aggressively didn't have *thoughts* about the future, either, punch, punch, punch. Beaverton was where I stopped pretending and started punching.

As soon as the summer between ninth grade and tenth grade ended, it became a blank in my memory, a whole month of it, at least, and though at the time I wasn't aware I had been blocking memories most of my life, I did, in the months after the summer, notice the absence of the forgotten month from my memory—I developed an aversion to going to school more comprehensive and more emotionally violent than any I had felt before and any I would feel after. Tenth grade seemed a more permanent development than ninth grade had—no matter what happened, no matter where my grandmother and I moved, I wouldn't find myself a tenth grader in middle school anywhere. While I was a ninth grader, my childhood had ended when I transferred from Whitford Middle School to Livermore High School, and had started up again when I transferred from Livermore High School to Five Oaks Middle School. But, despite my newly intensified aversion to going to school, I don't remember anything about my first days as a sophomore at Aloha High School.

Except I remember my favorite song at the time, and I think it was my first favorite song, though I had loved music intensely since I discovered *You're Living All Over Me* by Dinosaur Jr. when I was twelve or thirteen—I heard "Sludgefeast," the third song on their second album, *You're Living All Over Me*, in the first skate video I ever saw, and maybe I even owned the VHS tape, maybe I had rented the video and then copied it, we had two VCRs, *Ohio Skateout*, it was a skate video only in the sense that it was for most of its running time a video of people skateboarding, but it was a video of a skate contest, it wasn't a skate video in the contemporary sense. The song was "Knock Me Down" by the Red Hot Chili Peppers. Something about the song's message, largely, though imperfectly, summed up by the chorus, "If you see me getting mighty, if you see me getting high, knock me down," appealed to me, each time I heard the song, as if the song were speaking directly to me, though I wasn't mighty, though I had stopped trying to get high years before, though I didn't want to be knocked down anymore. And I remember listening to the song in the Aloha High School cafeteria, I must have brought my Walkman to school—a cassette Walkman, I wouldn't own a CD player until years later, though I did buy one CD months before I bought or was given a CD player, *Wings of Joy* by Cranes, after hearing a snippet of "Tomorrow's Tears" on MTV's *120 Minutes*, which I had programmed my VCR to record, since it was broadcast at midnight, the singer's voice, I thought when I first heard the song, sounded as if it were coming from inside me, the singer's voice sounded like a weeping child's voice—I remember listening to "Knock Me Down" in the cafeteria during what might have been my first week at Aloha High School, I remember listening to the song and wondering how I had lived so long, I was fourteen years old, how had I lived to be so old and who would knock me down next.

EXCEPT I REMEMBER—THESE THINGS must have happened in my first days at Aloha High School, at least during my first month there—sitting at the back of a classroom, leaning back in my chair, not tilting the chair back as I leaned, the chair was

attached to a desk, but trying to press myself through the wall behind my chair, through the back of the chair, as a redheaded
teacher, I don't remember his face but I remember his hair, his
face a few inches from my face, screamed at me about my lack of
effort, my lack of any effort at all, I hadn't turned in a single assign-
ment, though how could he have gotten so frustrated so quickly?
Maybe that didn't happen during my first month at Aloha High
School. Maybe it happened at the end of my first semester. But I
know the girl who screamed at the sight of me screamed at the
sight of me during my first month, more or less, at Aloha High
School, because she screamed at the sight of me about a week before I wrote my first poem, which I wrote on October 25, 1990. I
was standing in a hallway outside of a classroom, and the hallway was full, and so probably I had just exited the classroom, and
a girl was walking toward me, but she wasn't looking forward, her
face was turned to the side, she had the teased-up, tall hair that
was popular then, her hair looked almost like a bird's nest at its
peak, half a bird's nest, not a complete circle but a half circle, half
a bird's nest on its side, but not so dense as a bird's nest, it looked
more like the skeleton of a bird's nest, the ruin of a bird's nest, but
the look was popular then. She must have been talking to somebody, but I don't remember anybody walking beside her, and just
before she got close enough to me that she might have walked
into me, she turned to face me, not, I think, on purpose to face me,
but facing me was a result of her turning, and, seeing me, she
screamed. How sad I felt then, thinking, because I was fifteen, it
was my fate, I might even have thought the word "doom," but no,
that's a word I would use now if I were trying to imitate my

fifteen-year-old self, I would use it now were I attempting to portray what I was like when I was fifteen even though I know I wouldn't have used it then, thinking it was my fate to frighten people because my face was so ugly, diseased, my acne was so bad, how sad I felt then.

Except

I

Except I hadn't remembered, until three years ago when someone I had just met looked it up for me, why hadn't it occurred to me to look it up myself in the almost thirty intervening years? until three years ago I hadn't remembered the title of the movie I watched at school as part of an anti-suicide campaign, on October 25, 1990, the 590th anniversary of the death of Chaucer, as well as John Berryman's seventy-sixth birthday, though Berryman was in 1990 as dead as Chaucer, though younger in his death, the movie was called *Silence of the Heart*, it was a made-for-TV movie first released in 1984, and the movie in which Charlie Sheen made his acting debut, nor had I remembered the details of the plot, except I remembered the method of the protagonist's suicide, he drove his car off a cliff, and I remembered that after his suicide his sister read— at school, over the PA system or via a live video feed (even now I resist checking), in defiance of the principal, or the vice principal, or some other administrative figure, or merely a menacing adult—Sylvia Plath's "Lady Lazarus," not the whole poem, but lines in which I discovered the rest of my life:

Dying

Is an art, like everything else.

I do it exceptionally well.

II.

In a conversation with Thomas Higginson that took place on August 16, 1870, Emily Dickinson is reported to have said: "If I read a book [and] it makes my whole body so cold no fire ever can warm me I know *that* is poetry. If I feel physically as if the top of my head were taken off, I know *that* is poetry. These are the only way I know it. Is there any other way?" When I first heard the lines from "Lady Lazarus," I hadn't read Dickinson's definition of poetry—I hardly knew who Dickinson *was*, though I probably had encountered at least the opening lines of her poem beginning "Because I could not stop for Death," teens love that poem, it bounces off the walls in high schools from room to room. But when I first heard the lines from "Lady Lazarus," I felt as if the top of my head were being taken off.

III.

Except I remember I was depressed. When I was fourteen I wanted to be depressed and I wanted to look depressed, and when I was fifteen I wanted to be depressed and I wanted to look depressed, and maybe when I was fourteen and fifteen I actually *was* depressed, but I don't think I was. After my grandfather left—after my grandmother and I left my grandfather—my emotional life changed significantly, though I don't recall committedly inhabiting any particular emotional landscape, but only strongly wishing I inhabited certain emotional landscapes, really just depression. I wore all black and sought out music that seemed sad to me, though I hadn't yet developed a sense of what sad music was—for example, I found the debut album by The Charlatans, *Some Friendly*, relentlessly sad, bleak even, an appealing trudge, because of the moody vagueness of some of the lyrics, but now it strikes me as a not inordinately morose semi-psychedelic dance-pop album, unusual mostly for how catchy the songs are, hook after hook after hook, and it's something like happiness, a flash of happiness, though irritation can follow the flash, when a song's hook tears into one's mind— because I wanted to look sad and feel sad, and that's all I thought depression was, extended sadness, because I wanted anybody who saw me and anybody who spoke to me to think, "Wow, he is depressed," because to be sad seemed to me an act of notable rebellion, and to be depressed seemed to me a state of notable revolution, possibly because I was raised by white people who had been teens in the optimistic, for white people, 1950s.

But I didn't live, and hadn't lived before, though I was raised by white people who had been teens in the 1950s, in an oppressively happy home. My grandmother and grandfather had never attempted to trick the neighbors into thinking we were a happy family, and neither of them, as far as I knew, had ever pretended to be happy for my benefit. They never pressured me to be, or even to seem, happy. The sadness, the depression, that I wanted to signify was one side of a conversation I wanted to have with strangers. To anybody who saw me and anybody who spoke to me I wanted to seem like somebody they should try to save—a kidnapped child's rebellion, a kidnapped child's revolution, is to seem to strangers to need help—though at the time I didn't know that was what I wanted. After my grandfather left—after my grandmother left my grandfather and I left with her—my emotional life changed significantly not because I was sad he was gone, not at all, even at the time I felt immeasurably happy about his absence, but because I felt, though I couldn't have articulated this then, I felt I had halfway escaped my kidnappers, and so I joyously sought a way to signify to others that I needed help getting the rest of the way free, and so I wanted to look depressed, to *be* depressed. Black clothes, white socks. I wanted strangers to be so struck by my revolutionary depression, by my incongruity with the world, my war against the world, that they wouldn't be able to get me out of their minds. I wanted to make depression both my art and my cry, just as the speaker of "Lady Lazarus" makes dying her art and her cry.

IV.

Except I remember the day I heard those lines from "Lady Lazarus" I wrote eight poems. When I was a small child, I might have been six, I might have been seven, in the second or third grade, I loved Shel Silverstein's *Where the Sidewalk Ends*, which was an exceedingly popular book during my first years at Forest North, and consequently difficult to find at the school library. However, I remember repeatedly adding my name to the wait list for the book, and checking it out several times. Reading *Where the Sidewalk Ends*, never front to back, instead I would flip the book open and read whatever page was before me, or I would flip the book open, decide I didn't want to read the page before me, and thumb through the book until I found a poem I *did* want to read, reading *Where the Sidewalk Ends* was my first encounter with poetry, my first voluntary encounter with poetry, who knows, does she still remember? whether my mother read poetry to me when I was an infant, a toddler, who knows whether my father read poetry to me when I was an infant, a toddler, whether the night before my grandparents kidnapped me my father read me a rhyming children's story, what would he remember of those days? the last days, except the final moments, he remembers the final moments, and the long moment after, days filled by a long scream—reading *Where the Sidewalk Ends* was my first encounter with poetry, as far as I know, and in the eight or nine years between reading those poems and hearing the lines from "Lady Lazarus," I had no significant encounter with any other poems. Before I heard the lines from "Lady Lazarus," my understanding of poetry was so underdeveloped that when I attempted, a week or so before I heard the lines, I think on the day the girl in the hall screamed at the sight of me, when I attempted, because my feelings had been hurt and I needed a way to say my feelings, when I attempted to write a poem, not my first poem, but an attempted poem *before* my first poem, I started it with

Roses are red,

Violets are blue

because I thought that was how poems were supposed to start.

But the first poem I wrote in response to hearing Plath's lines didn't start with roses and violets, though I don't remember its first lines. I don't remember anything about those first poems, except that the first poem I wrote was called "Death Is an Art," and it ended painfully, with the line "And the artist is me," and that I also wrote a poem called "Happy" that began

This poem is happy,

So don't think it's funny

which even at the time I recognized as a somewhat forced distinction. I would say I had a below average amount of talent for writing poems, but having said so I would immediately want to correct what I had said, and say instead, in an effort to be both more specific and more honest, I had a *negative* amount of talent for writing poems, I would want to say that whatever occupied the space in me where talent ought to have been functioned like a black hole, from which no good line of poetry, not even a line good for a fifteen-year-old, could escape. But the people to whom I showed my early poems, friends at first, but eventually, after my grandmother and I moved to Salem, even though I still refused to do any schoolwork, teachers, too, never my grandmother, never my mother, the people to whom I showed my early, incompetent poems were encouraging. Now it seems to me they must have been amazed I was putting effort into something, and hoped only to encourage the effort itself. Now it seems to me they must have been relieved to see evidence something inside of me was still alive.

V.

Except I remember I had been given a test to evaluate my academic ability in the weeks before I first heard the lines from "Lady Laza-rus." All my life—can one use the phrase "all my life" when one is referring to oneself as a fifteen-year-old? Maybe when one actually *is* fifteen years old, but thirty years after the fact the phrase strikes one as ridiculous—all my life, even during the years since I had given up on my life and on school, I had been proud of my skill at taking standardized tests. When I was a small child I considered myself a competitive test-taker, especially with regard to standard-ized tests—whenever a standardized test was given, I made sure I finished the test before any other student in the room, slamming my pencil down loudly after I bubbled in my final answer, then scanning the room to catch any reactions on the faces of my peers, or, even better, on the face of my teacher. But it was also important to me that I got more answers correct than my peers did, though most of the time I couldn't be sure I had done so because we weren't usually told our individual scores. Every so often, however, we would be given a test, the results of which we *were* told, that deter-mined each student's ability compared to the average student in their grade as well as average students in grades above and below theirs. All my life, even during the years since I had given up on my life and on school, whenever I had taken such a test I had scored well above my grade level in every subject. But in the days before I heard the lines from "Lady Lazarus," almost two months into my sophomore year of high school, I was told my most recent performance on such a test indicated I was writing at an eighth-grade level. I remember thinking I would show them, whoever they were, I would prove I was smarter than that. Almost immediately I started writing the worst poems any fifteen-year-old had ever written.

VI.

Except I remember I wrote my first eight poems and the poems after those in a pocket-sized Mead notebook, the kind with the spiral wire that holds the pages together at the top, with a bright yellow cover, until I filled it.

VII.

Except I remember even then I felt I was discovering what my life might be. It didn't look familiar to me, but in a sense it was already mine, the journey toward it was mine—even in its unfamiliarity, I recognized it, my possible future life, I recognized the feeling of being unfamiliar with my life, like waking from a dream so vivid you feel bewildered in your own bed. When I was fifteen, the feel-ing of being unfamiliar with my life, a feeling that had followed me for as long as I could remember, began to guide me toward my life. When I was fifteen, I began to live inside poetry, having heard lines that began, as my life had begun, with dying.

The Tricycle

What color would the bike have been? Red, I think—the first thought I have in answer to the question is "It was red," and I see the glittering, deep, metallic red of a brand-new tricycle, the red of a metal apple. A tricycle, not a bicycle, and not a Big Wheel, my father might have given me a Big Wheel instead, which when I was a child was both the Lamborghini Countach and the Ford Pinto of three-wheeled vehicles, though Big Wheels didn't explode. But was that story ever more than a rumor, Pintos exploding? It now seems to me like the sort of story teenage boys tell each other in order to pretend they understand the world, in order to understand the world. It now seems to me like the sort of story teenage boys tell each other when they are beginning to understand that the world is often and in many ways ordered to gratify large, overage teenage boys pretending they understand the world.

Wikipedia tells me Pintos *did* explode, their fuel tanks having been positioned in a vulnerable spot—the thing meant to keep them going was placed in the wrong place, so either it kept them going or it set them on fire. The bicycle, the tricycle, the Big Wheel my father gave me just before my grandparents kidnapped me might have been red—they took me from his arms, I see myself reaching back, or they lifted me from the bicycle, the tricycle, the Big Wheel, I see myself reaching back. The thing meant to keep me going had been given to me by the wrong person, brief joy my fuel, and so the bicycle, the tricycle, the Big Wheel set me on fire.

Does knowing what causes explosions equal understanding the world? I don't understand the world. But I suspect knowing what set one on fire is more often than not the beginning of understanding. I think it was red, the vehicle my father gave me, so it was probably a tricycle—I remember, or imagine I remember, being lifted by my grandmother from something red like the fruit at the beginning of death.

SALEM THE FRUIT
AT THE BEGINNING OF
DEATH AND LIFE

The year and a half, was it? or could it have been longer? I can't imagine it was longer than a year and a half, but could it have been unimaginably long? the year and a half I lived in Beaverton has since become a knot of time in my memory, looping around and through itself. I know I didn't live there very long, and yet I feel as if I lived there from birth until I was fifteen and my grandmother and I moved to Salem—my memories of Beaverton play in my mind like a gif of a stalk of wheat being shaken by a breeze, looping seamlessly so that one can't tell whether the stalk is swaying in a relentless but gentle wind, or only leans forward once and returns once, the loop beginning again at the instant of the stalk's return to its original position. Why this should be so, I don't know, except what is being fifteen to a fifteen-year-old except almost being old enough to be sixteen? and so old enough to get a driver's license, and so old enough to start leaving one's home forever? If a memory loop, a knot of time, is going to be created in one's memory at any age, fifteen and seventeen, when one is almost old enough to be eighteen, would seem the most likely ages. In my mind, I lived in Beaverton for all I knew of forever until I was fifteen, just before I turned sixteen.

Just before I turned sixteen, my grandmother and I moved to Salem, a little over forty miles south of Beaverton. The last few months we had lived in Beaverton, maybe the whole of my last semester there, my grandmother was ostensibly homeschooling me—she had finally noticed my failing grades and had decided I needn't go to school if I wasn't going to try at school; she had decided, since we were going to move to Salem anyway, we might as well scrap my first attempt at tenth grade and start my sophomore year over in a new city. I don't know whether it occurred to her that, because she was requiring me to repeat the tenth grade, she was requiring me to live again a usually one-time-only part of life, to redo a year of my life, to step back in time, in the city from which she kidnapped me twelve years before, but I also don't know whether it ever occurred to her that she kidnapped me. We moved to Salem and turned back the outermost edge of a twelve-year-wide explosion by a year, and we ourselves stepped closer to the heart of the explosion. But did it occur to my grandmother to check whether my father still lived in Salem? If the last time you visited a certain midsized city you kicked a dog hard, maybe you were drunk, maybe you were just mean, but you've grown and changed since then, when you returned twelve years later you would remember the dog, you would feel heavy as you entered the city, and heavier still as you drove past the yard in which you kicked the dog. But to my grandmother, my father mattered less than a dog.

My grandmother and I moved to Salem to be closer to my grandmother's family—my family, too, they must have been my family, too, and they must still be my family, some dead now, some divorced now, some little changed from the people they were then, thirty years older, but little changed, people who live in houses the doors of which would open were I to knock on them, still, twenty years since I saw any of my grandmother's family. Her brother lived in Salem still, or had returned to Salem some time before after some years away, and his children lived in Salem still, or had returned to Salem some time before after some years away— I never discovered how many relatives on my grandmother's side lived in Salem still, but the city seemed stuffed with them, none downtown, in the city's heart, but at its fingertips, just before its fingertips stopped and the farmland and patches of forest reasserted themselves. We moved into a sky-blue manufactured home my grandmother would years later paint cotton-candy pink while she was in the midst of losing her mind.

We moved into a manufactured home but the house was built around our coming, some term other than "moving in" ought to capture moving into a house that wouldn't exist if one weren't moving into it, the house built to order, and it was the kind of house in which, during one's first weeks of occupancy, one finds oneself, as if by compulsion, again and again asserting its niceness to anybody else who lives in it, begging, with each assertion, for an assenting response. As we had in Beaverton, in Salem we lived in a cul-de-sac; as had been the case when my grandmother, my grandfather, and I arrived in Round Rock, much of our corner of the neighborhood wasn't there when we arrived. The rest of the neighborhood was at least a decade older than our corner, and none of it was manufactured homes, it was all whatever the opposite of a manufactured home is called, a home, it was all homes, luxuriously immobile brick, not every home brick, but every home could have been brick, every home immobile. The street on which we lived was new, houses were arriving every month, every week for a few weeks, the sidewalks were new, the edges of the curbs both too hard and too sharp, the concrete too bright. From the windows in the side of our house that faced the street, I could see, across the street, across an empty lot, over fences, the backs of the houses in the older rest of the neighborhood, compared to which our house, our manufactured home, looked like a simulation. The interior doors in our house were slightly, but noticeably, narrower than the interior doors in a whatever the opposite of a manufactured home is called, the front door slightly, but noticeably, wider, and all the doors, wooden interior, metal front, felt thin, felt light, felt cheap. My grandmother had chosen the optional, detached two-car garage, and only a few days after we arrived, I built an eight-foot-wide, two-foot-high quarterpipe in it with wood I stole from a nearby, seemingly abandoned, construction site, so I would have somewhere to skate on rainy days. But the garage was too small to allow me to build up the necessary speed to reach the top of the ramp with the garage door closed, so the ramp was only skateable, and then just barely, our driveway being somewhat steep, the ramp was only skateable on dry days, when the garage door was open. I would have to start pushing in the street, my back facing the backs of the immobile homes, toward the simulation, and keep pushing, hard, till just before I reached the ramp, worn out before I reached the ramp.

We arrived in dust, the new asphalt of the cul-de-sac caked and softened by dust from where? nowhere visible—from the previous emptiness of the place itself, now invisible because our house, at least, was there. But as had been the case when we arrived in Beaverton, when we arrived at our house in Salem, a skate ramp—this time a quarterpipe, and positioned on flat ground, pushed against the curb next to a lot upon which the construction of a house had started, but had stopped not long after it started—was near our new house, just past the intersection of the main road and the cul-de-sac, San Francisco Drive, upon which our house teetered (like the other manufactured homes soon to arrive in the neighborhood, our house appeared to have a cinderblock foundation, but the foundation was an illusion—before thin, sky-blue two-by-sixes were installed to hide it, a gap of about two inches was visible between the cinderblocks and the bottom of the house; whatever held the house up was invisible, hidden by the darkness beneath the house, the real darkness beneath the sky-blue simulation). We arrived in early sun, and as soon as I had carried into the house whatever I had to carry from the car, and had glanced at the rooms, noticing immediately the narrow doors, I skated over to the ramp and tested it, rolling up to and over the coping at the top of the ramp, pushing my front wheels down with my front foot after my front wheels passed over the top, while leaning slightly back, and then rolling backward down the ramp, discovering as I did so that the ramp was flimsier than it had appeared to be from the car. But only its existence, which indicated the nearby presence of other skaters, mattered to me.

But whoever the skaters were, I never found them, and one morning, not long after we arrived at our new house, I rolled over to the ramp to discover it had disappeared and left a not-quite-perfect almost rectangle of clean asphalt in the dust where it had stood, where it had leaned slightly.

MY FIRST DAYS IN SALEM, however long they were, days or weeks long, were lonely. I did eventually, after the ramp had disappeared, locate a skater deep in the neighborhood, amongst the immobile homes, a blond boy named James who had only been skating for a few months, and who was a year younger and at least half a foot shorter than me, but he claimed to have never even heard of the ramp. James and I skated together a few times, but skating didn't mean nearly as much to him as it meant to me, and because I, though I hadn't yet admitted it to myself at the time, was beginning to lose interest in skating (because skating, even when I skated alone, which I sometimes had done when I lived in Beaverton, and Raleigh Hills, and Livermore, was a social activity to me, and when I skated alone I was, at least in part, skating to get better at skating so I would be better at skating the next time I skated with my friends), his disinterest in skateboarding clashed with the great interest I professed, and emphasized uncomfortably the waning interest I felt. And James and I hung out together a few times, not skating, but the only thing that bound us together was skateboarding and proximity, and our friendship didn't last. But I never met anyone in Salem with whom I skated regularly, and no friendship I made there lasted long, though Salem was the last place I lived before I moved out on my own, I was eighteen then, by which time moving out was only moving out, I was too exhausted to escape my kidnapper, her mind already disappearing, though she would live another twelve years, and I left home like any child raised in the home to which they were born.

B ut I was skating with friends in Salem when I found my father. My memory of the day makes no sense to me, though I have tried almost every day for a year now to fit its parts together in a way that seems possible, a way that makes what I remember happening seem like it could have happened. No improbable coincidence set my father before me—I chose to discover him, though I had hated him for most of my life. But I remember being with friends who couldn't have been with me, in a place I couldn't have been—I remember skating with Aaron and Mark in an apartment complex in Beaverton, and stopping to look my father up in a stranger's phone book. But my father didn't live in Beaverton, he lived in Salem, so I couldn't have looked him up in a Beaverton phone book. But if I looked him up in Salem, in a Salem phone book, how were Aaron and Mark both with me? Mark visited once but I didn't look my father up during that visit, and I don't remember Mark visiting again, and I don't remember Aaron visiting ever. The memory exists in shards in my mind, shards orbiting a darkness, the shards make a sphere, like a bubble, but a sphere of disconnected fragments, through the cracks between which the darkness is visible, and seeps out, and whatever actually happened the day I found my father I can't see, and almost certainly I will never know it again. I can only tell what I now remember, though it couldn't have happened the way I remember it, what I remember was impossible, though I found my father in the midst of the impossible.

EITHER I FOUND MY FATHER in the summer or on a week-end. The impossible I remember makes the most sense if I found him in the summer, the summer just before I turned seventeen, though I remember being sixteen and knowing him longer than the few months possible if I had met him in the summer just before I turned seventeen. But I remember finding him in unfettered time, not the few cramped days of a weekend, and a weekend doesn't seem long enough for a visit from both Aaron and Mark, though I know they couldn't have been with me when I found my father, and surely if they had been with me their visit wouldn't have been longer than two days and one night. But if Aaron and Mark were with me, then I found my father either late in the afternoon or fairly early in the morning, not too early, ten or so, since Aaron and Mark would probably have arrived in the early afternoon, and left in the early afternoon the next day. Since my memory will not accommodate their absence, Aaron and Mark were with me when I found my father in the summer just before I turned seventeen, and the sun was low in the sky.

We had decided to skate somewhere we had never skated before, a newish apartment complex down the road from my house, a complex I can only picture as being maybe three-quarters of a mile, maybe a mile from my house in Beaverton, though when I found my father I was living in Salem. The complex had been built on uneven ground, and so its common areas featured many small sets of steps to ollie both down and up, and short handrails to slide and grind. The only trick I remember doing the day I found my father was a frontside 180 ollie to fakie nosegrind, a trick I never felt comfortable doing, but I never felt comfortable doing any of the three or four tricks I could eventually do down handrails, the vocabulary of known handrail tricks was small at the time, a frontside 180 ollie to fakie nosegrind down a short handrail was still cutting edge or near the cutting edge, though the handrail was short and my front truck barely made contact with its last few inches. But neither Aaron nor Mark could do the trick, and to us, to me, at least, though I can't know how they felt, the trick seemed almost miraculous, I did it and felt like I couldn't have done it, the impossibility I had first felt when I learned the trick months before had stayed with me, the impossibility both part of the trick and not part of the trick, the way Death's scythe is both part of Death and not. Though I don't remember any other trick any of us did, though I watched Aaron and Mark enthusiastically I don't remember any trick they did, I remember feeling more excited than I usually did watching them skate, though they couldn't have been there, and surely I felt unusually excited because I now had so few opportunities to skate with either of them—none, except once before with Mark, since I had moved to Salem the year before, though we couldn't have skated together on the day I found my father, though I felt unusually excited watching them skate that day.

We skated at the apartment complex for maybe ten minutes,

maybe fifteen, though by the time we finished I was sweating so profusely I must have looked like I had been skating there for hours. I don't remember a single thing Aaron and Mark and I ever talked about, besides asking each other whether we could go skating together, except I remember we once had an absurd conversation about sex while we stood in the street in front of my house in Beaverton, absurd because none of us knew anything about sex, but we had to talk with each other about sex lest we mistake each other for boys who knew nothing about sex, each of us affirming the delusions and lies of the other two, never again such joyous friendships, but maybe as we skated or after we skated I talked with them about wanting to find my father, maybe I talked with them about suspecting he still lived in Salem, I had heard about the Mc-Crae family at school, certain teenage members of which were only spoken of in whispers, though they didn't go to my school, McKay High School, the name so close to my father's last name, the one name I was sure about, my father Stan Lee McCrae or Stanley Mc-Crae. Maybe they encouraged me to look for him. Maybe I said OK, I'll do it, I'll find him right now, let's knock on somebody's door and ask to borrow their phone book, and maybe they said yeah, man, do it, I can't imagine not telling them what I was about to do before I knocked on the door of one of the apartments at the edge of the complex, more a duplex than an apartment, not connected to any of the large, multi-apartment buildings, but painted with the same color scheme, one of several duplexes at the edge of the complex. I knocked on the door and a young white woman with slightly longer than shoulder-length straight hair the shade of brown I've always called blond and a baby on her hip answered it,

240

and I took a breath, and the breath I took in seemed to enter me through my mouth, through my eyes, and through my ears, and I said, "Hi. I'm sorry to bother you, but could I use your phone book?" And the woman looked at Aaron and Mark, both standing behind me, one behind the other on the narrow walk, then looked again at me, sweating like I had been skating for hours, but sweating like I had been running toward her door for thirteen years, wouldn't I have gotten stronger, used to the running, in all those years? and she said, "Sure," and waved me and Aaron and Mark into her shadowy apartment, but the shadows were blue, and like the clothing of light.

The day I found my father might have been the day I broke my ankle, ollie to feeble stall, the ledge about fourteen inches high, I leaped from the ground to do a simple trick, a trick I had done dozens of times before, it was hardly a trick at all, I had found my father dozens of times before in my head, always vengefully, and though I didn't find my father the day I broke my ankle, I might have found him on that day, the vengefulness having begun to disappear from my mind. As I approached the ledge, I hadn't committed to doing any particular trick, the trick was ollieing high enough that one wouldn't ollie all the way over the obstacle, but would lock one's back truck on the obstacle's edge, the trick *looked* like a trick not all the way done, a trick to which one hadn't committed before doing it, unless one leaned back stylishly, twisted one's body backward, and looked back, but I hadn't committed to turning stylishly away, but had only landed briefly in a feeble stall, hardly a stall, if somebody had photographed me at exactly the right instant, in the photograph I would have looked like I were in a feeble stall, but my body language would look wrong, I would look as if I were beginning to turn the board away from the edge, not backward, in the stylish direction, but forward, completing the motion I had begun when I turned my board slightly in the air so that my back truck would land on the ledge, my body slumping downward in such a way as to suggest the turning. The photograph would be a photograph of falling, me falling ridiculously from a throwaway trick, and the fall wasn't hard, and it couldn't have looked serious, I didn't hit the ledge on the way down, but I twisted my ankle beneath me, and I knew immediately my ankle was broken, and I told Aaron and Mark, immediately, my ankle was broken, and whoever, Aaron or Mark, but I think it was Mark, was about to do the next trick stood up straight, who had been crouching slightly, thoughtfully, in anticipation of his next trick, and whoever was standing next to him, Aaron or Mark, but I think it was Aaron, stepped toward me and asked, "What should we do?" and I told him I had to go home, and I said I didn't know how I would get home, I couldn't walk, and I couldn't skate, and Aaron or Mark said, "Sit on your board and we'll push you," and they did, they pushed me from behind the building, a grocery store, they rolled me past the weeds, over the asphalt, and onto the sidewalk, and once we were on the sidewalk they had to push me uphill, both Aaron and Mark were smaller than me, Aaron smaller than Mark, but they pushed me together, and they took turns pushing me, and I helped, I tried to help, pulling myself forward with my hands, I might have looked, were an observer focusing their attention entirely upon me, I might have looked as if I were climbing the hill, one hand after the other, but I couldn't have climbed it, I was being pushed up the hill. How, without Aaron and Mark behind me, could I have gotten home? In my memory of the day I found my father, Aaron and Mark and I were together in the town where we had once spent forever together, they were standing behind me as I stood at the door of a room in which the shadows looked like the clothing of light.

The day I found my father might have been my first day at Five Oaks, my first day at the third school I attended in the ninth grade. I might have stepped from the counselor's office and seen him working at a desk across from her door, I don't know what work he was doing when I was fourteen—he might have been employed in that office, or he might have worked repairing office machinery. I wouldn't have known him if I had seen him. I might have, as I sat across from the counselor, she behind her desk, nothing in front of me, I might have, as I scanned the room, my eyes flitting from the poster on the wall, maybe a poster on the wall—not the poster of the kitten clinging with both paws to a rope sometimes, sometimes clinging with one paw to a length of string, always above the phrase "Hang in there," but a poster like it, the same spirit—to the prize ribbons for what, to the picture of maybe the counselor's daughter, a girl with a horse, to the door, on the other side of which my father sat at a desk in a group of desks in a large, open space. I might have heard him typing, the effortless, electric typewriters common then, the throbbing hum always seemingly the sound of too much power for a machine that had functioned manually, no power but fingers, for decades, the tap of the ball against the platen like the tap of a walking stick against a linoleum floor, the person holding the cane walking too fast, running, running from what, I might have heard him during the short silence between the last calm thing she said and her almost shout, "Look me in the eyes when I'm talking to you," or I might have heard him during the longer, deeper silence, the room now vulnerable to the faintest sound from anywhere near, between her almost shout and my reply, the silence longer though I replied before the surprise, the almost shock, filled my chest, the effortless, overpowered, electric typewriters common then, made by the company for which my grandfather worked, each typewriter heavier than it looked, probably too heavy for me to lift then, though when had I ever touched one? my grandfather worked with computers. How many IBM Selectric typewriters did my father touch during the years of my absence without recognizing the connection between the machine and my grandfather? How many IBM PCs? None? Two or three? Every typewriter, every personal computer, he ever touched? He might have been outside the door, he might have been in Salem, he never moved from Salem, he told me the day we met, thinking I would come back, he might have been fifty miles from where I was, missing by then eleven years, most of those years thousands of miles away, the room vulnerable to the slightest sound.

The day I found my father might have been a day on the drive from Round Rock to Livermore, impossible, me, my grandparents, and John, the youngest son of family friends. My grandparents had no other friends in Round Rock I ever met, how many people could they trust? Except once we spent New Year's Eve at a party at the house of a family I don't remember seeing again and hadn't met before, no other children in the house, and someone gave me a flute of champagne, I was eight or nine, but I already knew I hated the taste of alcohol, how many people could my grandparents trust? Had they noticed my habit of declaring I didn't have a father and I hated him? Had they noticed I had lived my whole life with them saying the same impossible thing? How many people could they trust not to ask questions? If John's parents knew my grandparents had kidnapped me, did they worry about sending him halfway across the country with us, all of us together in a van? But if John's parents knew my grandparents had kidnapped me from a black man, would they have worried? We might have passed my father, all of us together in a van, we might have passed him on a freeway somewhere between Round Rock and Livermore, my father has family in Arizona, I have family in Arizona, and my father had wanted to take me to Arizona just before my grandparents kidnapped me, he had delayed the trip to let them take me for a weekend, a thirteen-year-long weekend, surely he traveled to Arizona more than once, surely he traveled to Arizona many times, in the years I was gone, we might have passed him, he might have been on the other side of a semitruck on a wide freeway as John and I signaled to the driver to blow the truck's horn, each of us pulling an imaginary string down, each of us raising his arm to return the string to its original position, then pulling it down again, our fists balled as if we were punching the sky, my father might have been on the other side of the truck when the driver blew the horn, my father might have jumped in his seat, though I've never seen him startled, he might have been, for a moment, afraid, he might have wondered where the danger was, me, and John, and my kidnappers, all of us together, impossible, in a van on the other side of the semi screaming beside him, the driver always blew the horn twice, my father might have cursed, the first chance he had in eight years to be angry with me, though I've never known him to be angry with me.

The day I found my father might have been the night before my mother's parents took me from him forever, for the next thirteen years of forever, four times longer than I had been alive, four times what I knew of forever, by then of course I was talking, of course I was walking. When I was a child my grandmother liked to tell me I had talked and walked early, both more than two years before she kidnapped me, though of course she never framed her stories that way, or I liked to ask her how old I was when I first talked and walked, but now only remember her answering, but to whom did I talk? to whom did I walk? The only person I know who can still describe clearly an instance of me talking and walking when I was younger than three, running, he says I ran to him, is my father, that I would run to him in the night to wake him, but I wasn't afraid, it was a game, and he was usually already awake, though in bed, I was two, he says, me emerging from the dark, though I had already been close, my bed was in the same room as his, and leaping onto his bed, me emerging from the dark as if I had been waiting in the dark, when your child makes a habit of a game how long do you expect your child will play it? months? years? how long do you expect your child will play it before your child disappears? you lying in the dark, you haven't been able to sleep for days, not since your child disappeared, you are in the middle of the game still, was my father in the middle of the game still when I was told not to leap onto my mother's parents' water bed? I had, how long after they kidnapped me? run across the wide chasm of the living room in Round Rock, suspended above the largest network of caves in Texas, turned just before the doorframe beyond which, three, four years later, I would see the Devil, regained my speed and jumped onto their bed—did the game end when I hit the bed and woke them? Did the game end when they told me to never do that again? My mother's parents had hidden the room in which my father and I had slept, the darkness in which again and again I had discovered my father. Did the game end when my father stopped expecting me to emerge from the dark as if I had been waiting in the dark? He says I would put my forehead against his forehead so I could see, in the darkness, whether his eyes were open. Could I stay awake? Discovering my father in the darkness was discovering myself. My mother's parents had hidden that darkness beneath another, incommensurate darkness, the largest network of caves in Texas hidden beneath a house.

(My mother's mother didn't understand what I was doing, what I wanted, surely she didn't, when, after she had tucked me in and read me a story, I grabbed her face and pulled her forehead to mine, not the first time, not the second time, and I remember her, the first time? the second time? I see her recoiling in the near dark, a night-light shining from an outlet across the room, but was it the third time? the fourth time? eventually, she locked her eyes with mine and tilted her head from side to side, as she did so making an alarm-like sound, so that, as I tried to follow her eyes, I became dizzy, and giggled, and maybe she wondered then who had taught me to do this strange thing I hadn't done at all, the strange thing *she* had done, at which I had giggled, my father? but more likely she wondered whether my mother had taught me to do the strange thing, how often did my mother's mother think about my father in those first weeks after she kidnapped me? more often than she ever would again? only at moments when I seemed inexplicable, as I had when I first pulled her white face toward my black face? or not at all, not at all? or maybe my mother's mother just felt relieved and then stood from my bed and turned to go, having given me what I had seemed to want.)

Aaron and Mark and I stood in the stranger's dim living room, her vertical blinds nearly closed, we stood in blue shadows that looked like the clothing of light. The stranger—but how could she have been a stranger here, in her own living room?—never asked for our names, and we never asked for hers, she kept herself strange to us, and we kept ourselves strange to her, the stranger set her baby down in a playpen near the sliding glass door at which the vertical blinds indecisively filtered the late-afternoon sunlight, the playpen situated between a brown leather couch and a television, but to the side, so as not to interrupt the view of the television from the couch, the television perched atop a low entertainment center, blond wood, an open compartment on each side and a wide drawer between them, half as deep as the television itself. The stranger set her baby down in a playpen and pulled the phone book from the right-hand compartment of the entertainment center. She handed the book to me. I noticed then the white telephone, the size and shape of an office telephone, but with oversized buttons, on the small round table next to the couch, between the couch and the sliding glass door, but out of reach of the baby in his playpen, I noticed the phone, and it occurred to me the stranger might be expecting me to ask to use it, and I said, "Thanks. I just need to look up a number." The stranger stood a few feet away from me, between me and the television, watching as I flipped through the white pages. Since I was turned away from Aaron and Mark, facing the sliding glass door through which I couldn't see, the blinds pulled tight enough that no individual features of the outside world were visible, only the light, the stranger would have been the only person who saw the look on my face, if she was looking at my face, or nobody saw it, what does the expression at the end of thirteen years look like? the stranger would have been the only person who saw the look on my face when I spotted a name I thought could be my father's, "McCrae, S," not my name, my last name was my grandfather's last name then, no way to know whether my father's name was Stan Lee or Stanley. I saw his number. I slapped the phone book shut, handed it back to the stranger, thanked her, and left, Aaron and Mark behind me again, maybe I had rushed past them toward the front door. I felt strange reaching for the doorknob, like I shouldn't touch it, being a stranger in the house.

Days later, a Saturday afternoon, I called my father. I took the phone book, my grandmother's phone book, from the flimsy wooden table next to the couch in the living room, between the couch and the front door, I was sixteen. Five years later, six years later, my grandmother's Alzheimer's erupted from her, the early signs of which she was already showing, though I didn't recognize the signs, my mother didn't recognize the signs, her temperament had changed, her anger now, in the midst of arguments, would grow seemingly bigger than her body, and she would be driven by it from wherever in the house the argument was happening, always in the house, into her bedroom, slamming the door behind her, and I would have to beg for her to come back out, though she couldn't run anywhere from fights on the phone with my mother, who lived in Portland still, and instead my grandmother simply wouldn't speak to her at all for months at a time. My grandmother's Alzheimer's erupted, and the house she had dusted twice a day every day for years, as she had dusted the house before it, and the house before that, and the house before that, filled with garbage, a foot deep everywhere, every room in the house had burst its boundaries, and the table from which I took her phone book disappeared into a pile of the house's insides, the house itself vivisected by my grandmother's disease.

I took the phone book into my bedroom and quietly closed the door. I opened the white pages at *K*, then flipped to *M*, then to "McCrae, S," reached for my black telephone, the cheapest phone we could find at, where would it have been? Bi-Mart, probably, and dialed the number next to the name. The line rang once, and a woman answered, I remember thinking later that something in her voice sounded as if she had been waiting for my call, my own voice shaking even before I spoke. I said, "Hi. I'm trying to reach Stan . . . Lee McCrae."

The woman said, "Hold on," and set the receiver down.

And how long later I heard the sound of the receiver being picked up, a compressed shuffling, and I didn't have time to think all the way to the end of the thought "My father is picking up the phone," though I started to think it, then his voice, "Hello?" that I hadn't heard for thirteen years, immediately like no other person's voice—an accent I couldn't place, music from somewhere I didn't know anymore wavering in each syllable, even a simple word like "hello" loosened by music, made difficult to understand, though I knew he had said "Hello," though I had heard only music. And I asked him his name.

Acknowledgments

When it first occurred to me to write this book, I thought this book would be impossible to write. And it would have been impossible to write if my friends and family and agents (friends, too) and editors (friends, too) hadn't supported me while I was writing it. Because there's no measuring one's love for one's friends, I'll list them in alphabetical order. A lifetime of thank you to: Amy Acre, Timothy Donnelly, Jonathan Galassi, Alan Gilbert, Claire Gillespie, Derek Gromadski, Jake Wild Hall, Anastasios Karnazes, Dorothea Lasky, Joshua Mehigan, Bradford Morrow, Paul Muldoon, Deborah Paredez, Chris Richards, James K. A. Smith, Ellah Wakatama, G. C. Waldrep, Alice Whitwham, and Lynn Xu. And a lifetime of thank you to everyone at The Cheney Agency and at Scribner, friends and friends I haven't met yet. If by mistake I've left your name out, that is no sign of diminished love, but only an indicator of how bad my memory has become.

Because it helped me to think as I wrote this book, here is the Catherine Pickstock epigraph in its larger context, excerpted from

After Writing: On the Liturgical Consummation of Philosophy: "Resurrection is the process at work in non-identical repetition by which that which is repeated is not unmediably different, but analogously the same. This redemptive return is what allows a person to tell a story, since for there to be a story, there must be 'analogous' subjects and objects, persisting as same-yet-different. . . . And so every story is by definition a resurrection story."

Finally, I would like to thank my children, and I would like to thank Melissa McCrae, without whose love and support not only could I not be happy, I could not be.